*Not
Responsible
for
Personal
Articles*

LOIS GOULD

Not Responsible for Personal Articles

Random House　New York

My thanks to A. M. Rosenthal and Arthur Gelb, for their friendship and support

Copyright © 1973, 1974, 1975, 1977, 1978 by Lois Gould

All rights reserved under International and Pan-American Copyright Conventions. Published in the United States by Random House, Inc., New York, and simultaneously in Canada by Random House of Canada Limited, Toronto.

Portions of this book have appeared in *Cosmopolitan, New York* magazine, and *McCall's*.

"K.Y.S.L.O.O.T.O." was originally titled "The Story of Oogh," and "Confessions of a Health-Club Nut" was originally titled "How I Found Love in a Nautilus Time Machine." Both stories appeared originally in *New York* magazine.

Grateful acknowledgment is made to the following for permission to reprint previously published material:
The New York Times—for the following selections: "Women Have Stopped Taking Dictation"—Fashion of the Times Magazine (March 3, 1974); "Country Houses"—Times Book Review (June 10, 1973); "Good Manners for Liberated Persons"—Magazine (December 16, 1973); "Letter to a Robber"—Magazine (March 10, 1974); "Porn for Women; Women for Porn"—Magazine (March 2, 1975); "The Perfect Marriage"—Magazine (July 6, 1975). © 1973, 1974, 1975. For the collection of *HERS* articles. © 1977 by the New York Times Company.

Library of Congress Cataloging in Publication Data

Gould, Lois.
Not responsible for personal articles.

I. Women—United States—Social conditions—
Addresses, essays, lectures. 2. United States—
Social conditions—1960-   —Addresses, essays,
lectures. I. Title.
HQ1426.G68   301.41'2   77-13654
ISBN 0-394-42780-7

Manufactured in the United States of America
9 8 7 6 5 4 3 2
FIRST EDITION

For Tony, Roger and the B, with love
Also for Jane Rinzler, who is smart, strong and beautiful,
as befits the daughter of an action heroine

What is the matter with Mary Jane?
She's perfectly well, and she hasn't a pain,
And it's lovely rice pudding for dinner again!
What *is* the matter with Mary Jane?

—A. A. MILNE

Contents

Good Manners for Liberated Persons   3
The Perfect Marriage   17
Women Have Stopped Taking Dictation   21
How to Liberate Your Entire Family, in Your Own Home,
    Without Cost or Obligation   26
Guess Who's Not Coming to Dinner   35
The ERA Account   39
Leading Ladies   43
Trading Up   47
All Hair the Conquering Heroine   52
Unfair Sex at MIT   56
O Tempora! O Mores! O Prom!   61
K.Y.S.L.O.O.T.O.   66
Uncivil Liberties   71
Guilty as Charged   75
The Switching Hour   86
Court One   96

Under the Influence 95
Sanjay's Complaint: A Psychohistory Lesson 99
Mother Loving 103
Porn for Women; Women for Porn 106
Combat in the "Adult" Zone 121
City Mouse, Country House 126
Confessions of a Health-Club Nut 131
The Year of the Barbara 143
Letter to a Robber 147
Queasy Rider 155
Ms. Alliances 159

Not
Responsible
for
Personal
Articles

Good Manners for Liberated Persons

The whole relation of men to women, as far as etiquette is concerned, is based on the assumption that woman is a delicate, sensitive creature, easily tired, who must be fêted, amused and protected, and to whom the bright and gay side of the picture must always be turned.
—VOGUE'S BOOK OF ETIQUETTE, 1948

ETIQUETTE? THE VERY WORD IS SOME SPECIES OF JOKE. YOU MEAN which fork (spoon?) for the plum pudding, or how to address a limp asparagus at a holiday buffet? And what to do when the Toploftys cut you dead after New Year's Eve?

Well, no. What *I* mean by etiquette is what went on in my seventh-grade biology class. I was one of six girls admitted to a previously all-male public school, and the biology teacher had never before encountered a live female specimen in his classroom.

The first problem was his method of dispensing the textbooks. He had always just yelled out each boy's last name in alphabetical order and then hurled a book at him. Baxter? Thwack. Carnovsky? Thunk. Clearly a practice that would not do for young ladies.

He solved the problem by yelling out the boys' last names and hurling the books at them as usual and dropping his voice to a polite whisper whenever he came to a girl's name. *Miss* Lopez. And then he'd lope over to her seat to deliver her book by hand. Also, he blushed.

The most important aspect of this mortifying procedure was not the girls' embarrassment, nor even the boys' snickers. It was the biology lesson. Girls, we were taught, inside of one unforgettable hour, are innately special. Girls are to be "respected" for their girlness. And above all, girls are never to be treated like the rest of us. That's etiquette.

I have forgotten, or mercifully blocked, the name of that gentlemanly teacher, but I do remember that his deference extended all the way to the first marking period, when he passed one of the girls and told her that had she been a boy, he would have had to flunk her. Needless to say, every boy in the class heard about that, and detested us all for it. They probably would have detested us anyway, but I always thought it was etiquette that clinched it.

This may have been an extreme case, even for its time. Maybe now the teacher would at least flunk that girl. But I suspect he would still call her *Miss,* and still blush. Unfortunately, etiquette is alive and well in the age of liberation.

Back in 1953, *Esquire* published a more or less definitive etiquette guide for sophisticated men. In it were engraved the following basic wisdoms about how to relate to women:

"The man who believes everything a woman tells him needs more than an etiquette book to straighten him out. You want to take her at her word, but it's good manners *not* to when she says: 'Please don't get up; Please sit down; Don't bother—I can manage; You go ahead, I'll be all right.' (Your firm duty is to take care of her; she expects you to insist.)"

Esquire also noted wryly that modern woman may be "a past master at handling headwaiters or hailing taxis or squelching mashers when she's alone—but when she's with you, etiquette renders her helpless. You're *It*."

Nearly a generation later, in 1970, an etiquette guide for boys called *Male Manners* reported that nothing had changed. Girls "have a great urge to be taken care of," the editors advised. And on a list of the six most common complaints girls have about boys' behavior, "not helping girls with coats" ranked No. 3, right behind dirty language and bad table manners. For the record, No. 6 was "Not ordering for dates in restaurants," and there were thirty lesser, but still rankling, pet peeves, including "Not standing when ladies [sic] enter a room," "Not pulling out chairs for girls," "Not helping girls through crowds," "Not walking on the outside" and, finally, "Never giving compliments—especially when she spent hours making herself pretty for you."

Chances are not many teen-age boys were seriously into etiquette books in 1970—if ever. But on some level they must have gone on believing in the rules. Even as they were flouting them, even as girls everywhere were bitching (genteelly) about their flouting them, their biology teachers, or some other well-bred grownups (such as the publishers of etiquette books), were living by them. And now, in the midst of revolution, authority figures in general—from Amy Vanderbilt and the Emily Post Institute down to Abigail Van Buren and Dr. David Reuben—are still living by them. Home, motherhood and the nuclear family have all been attacked. But nobody has raised a pinkie against etiquette.

Isn't it time we considered, for instance, what a liberated social arbiter would deem proper in the following situations?

• Billie Jean King and Bobby Riggs are lunching at a restaurant. The waiter is about to present the check. Where should he put it? And why?

- Germaine Greer is about to demolish Norman Mailer on a TV talk show, when her cigarette goes out. Should he offer her a light? What if *his* cigarette goes out?
- At a dinner-dance, a girl who moves like early Ginger Rogers and thinks like late Gloria Steinem is seated next to a man with two left feet. He asks her for the last tango. Who leads?
- Sally Quinn interviews Henry Kissinger, and likes him. How can she let him know without creating the wrong impression? What *is* the wrong impression? And if the interview goes on till 2 A.M., should he offer to see her home? Even if she lives in Chevy Chase?
- After a heated debate at the House of Representatives, an angry congressman shouts a stream of explicit Anglo-Saxonisms in the cloakroom corridor. Should he apologize to Barbara Jordon? Why?
- Dr. Joyce Brothers and her husband are invited to a Christmas party. Should they be addressed as Dr. and Mrs. Milton Brothers? At what time of day does a woman stop wearing her Ph.D.?
- Princess Anne is "given" in marriage by her father, and promises to "obey" her husband. He in turn promises to "worship" her, in the sacred words of the traditional marriage ceremony. Meanwhile, in the United States, a less famous bride asserts her intention to keep her own name after marriage. Under her wedding photograph in the newspapers she is carefully identified as "Mrs. Whozit, the former Miss Soandso." Is there anything seriously wrong with any of this?

At first blush these questions may seem idle, if not downright trivial. But as Richard Duffy wrote in his 1922 introduction to Emily Post's historic *Etiquette,* which sold a million copies at the height of the Depression: "Trifles are unimportant, it is true, but then, life is made up of trifles."

Or, as any woman with a half-raised consciousness would put it in 1973, "This ain't just poli*tesse,* mister, it's poli*tics.*"

Money is the Root

Let us begin with the hypothetical King-Riggs lunch. We may safely assume that this is a business occasion. Despite the fact that women have been taking men to business lunches for years, etiquette still deems it somewhere between embarrassing and disgraceful for a woman to be seen paying a check. Especially if she pays cash. In 1954 Amy Vanderbilt fluttered: "In all cases, for the sake of the man, a woman tries to avoid a public display of her financial arrangements. Onlookers cannot know the circumstances, and men are easily embarrassed by a career woman's usurpation of their traditional role. Even if she is lunching a junior executive [or a defeated tennis rival], it is courteous to allow him the dignity of seeming to pay the bill. The arrangements for the preservation of male pride can be made in several ways. . . ."

And in 1969 the revised 12th edition of Emily Post's *Etiquette* discussed the same delicate problem, with obvious distaste. Mrs. Post's heirs felt strongly that if a woman must pay, she should at least have the decency to use a credit card (assuming she can get one; credit-card-company etiquette often involves saying "No" to women). "The act of signing a slip of paper," according to the latest *Etiquette,* "does not somehow seem so objectionable as having the woman . . . count out the money while the man sits helplessly by. In fact, this situation is so awkward that many women without charge privileges prefer to give their guest a sum of cash large enough to cover the bill before they enter the restaurant, thus relieving the man of any embarrassment before the waiter."

Does a strong man really flinch at the sight of a woman wielding a $20 bill? Does modern etiquette really boil down to a question of who is kidding whom? And why are men so terrified of waiters?

Somehow it seems like such a simple thing. Couldn't the waiter just put the check down in a neutral corner of the table and let Billie Jean or Bobby lob it—or, better still, split it?

Economic reality (most women still earn less than most men) may dictate that for nonexpense-account lunches or dinners, a woman won't be able to split the check every time. And if they're dining at the Ritz, perhaps no time. In that case, it seems logical that they should eat someplace cheaper. Or take turns treating, even if it means soyburgers at home once a week.

In Emily Post's day, a young lady "from a monied family" was sternly advised to adjust her rich tastes to her poor young man's pocketbook. For liberation's sake, I'd say, a monied man today ought to do the same. Otherwise we'll never get past that other old rule: "He [sic] who pays the piper calls the tune." Which is not just a rule of etiquette, but of (who is under whose) thumb.

Thank you, kind sir

Now, then, let's consider Norman Mailer's gentlemanly impulse to light Germaine Greer's cigarette. This issue is closely allied to many other forms of masculine assistance: holding coats, opening doors, carrying bundles, steering through crowds, giving up bus seats. In short, the lending of a strong male hand for the thousand tiny struggles that mark fragile woman's perilous existence.

From a feminist standpoint, this kind of gesture seems perfectly nonsexist, and indeed rather nice—on three conditions: (1) she really needs his help (he can tell she does if she asks for it, or if, when he offers, she says yes, thanks); (2) he readily accepts the same kind of help from her, or from any woman, when he needs it, and (3) she just as readily offers the same kind of help to him—or to another woman—without any of them worrying about what it's doing to her or his sexual image. The point is simply that no man should automatically hop around door-holding or chair-pulling or cigarette-lighting for a woman, as *Esquire* put it in 1953, "just as if she hadn't a muscle in her body." We all know she has muscles; why shouldn't she use them to open the door, for heaven's sake?

A man I know confided recently that he has always been inept at summoning taxis and forgetful about helping women in and out of them. Women used to consider him unmanly or rude or both. Now he's known as "politically aware."

If there is to be a new etiquette, it ought to be based on honest mutual respect, and responsiveness to each other's real needs. Regardless of sex. In other words, a man should certainly give up his seat to a woman who's carrying the groceries and the baby—and so should a woman, for a man who is so burdened. In the very near future, one fervently hopes, plenty of men in fact will be so burdened.

I won't dance; don't ask me

Now that social dancing has emerged from the touch-me-not stage of rock 'n' roll and reverted to its former glory as a body-contact sport, we've also exhumed the rigid mini-etiquette of the ballroom floor. Men are the leaders: One Ms.-step and you're out. Yet I know of at least one young couple who were miserable for years because she is a superb dancer and he is an ox, and who have finally reversed roles, breaking every rule in Arthur Murray's book. She leads, and he follows, and they claim to be having a ball. Literally. Every night in their own living room, and at least once a week in public. This alone may not save their marriage, but then again, who can tell? All I know is that a man who can't dance well should not automatically get to lead on a dance floor, and a woman who can should not have to follow. (Some purists might carp that if he's a six-footer and she's five foot two, it will look odd for her to lead—but how much odder than if she's a six-footer and he's five foot two and he's leading?) When they're equally skilled, Nureyev can certainly continue twirling Margot Fonteyn forever. But in the case of Ms. and Mr. Average Couple and the fox trot, the person who steps livelier ought to set the pace. If liberation doesn't fix this social injustice soon, I have a feeling that by 1984 the happy comeback of cheek-to-cheek will be all over. We'll be back to nothing but rock-'n'-roll democracy (no leaders, no followers and no touching), or else we will all end up sitting this one out.

Your place or mine?

Like social dancing, the dating game still operates by its own set of antique rules, none of which ought to apply in a liberated age, but most of which still do, indicating that either the age is not so liberated as some of us think, or else that *we* aren't. Men are still supposed to lead, pursue, initiate and make the first phone call. Women are still supposed to sit by the phone, smiling, and not sound too thrilled when it rings. If she's actually pursuing him, then, as in the restaurant game, she is still supposed to pretend she isn't. And in dating, it isn't just a waiter who has to be fooled, it's the man himself. This game has always been tricky at best, and profoundly immoral, but until now nobody ever questioned the propriety of it. It's time someone did. Test yourself:

If a woman compliments a man, or frankly says she likes or

admires him, is it a sexual invitation? Won't he think it is, even if she didn't mean it to be? If your answer to either of those questions is yes, you haven't come a long way, baby. (Note: Dr. Kissinger hasn't either. He still refers to women as a hobby.)

As for the custom of escorting a woman home—after any kind of late show—this tradition, too, seems in need of agonizing reappraisal. If she lives in an unsafe neighborhood, or feels uncomfortable going home alone, she ought to accept a man's offer to accompany her without feeling unliberated. On the other hand, if she does feel safe, she should say so, and he ought to accept that, without feeling his protector's role has been usurped again (or, worse, that he's been rejected sexually).

For that matter, how about the safety of a boy who lives in the Bronx, takes his girl friend home to Queens every night and then rides the subway home alone at 2 A.M.? In the old days he would have had three choices: stop dating her, take her home earlier, or get married. By now, one would hope they could figure out a few more choices. (One man I know solves the problem neatly by dating only married women. Etiquette thus frees him from both pickup and delivery.)

And speaking of sexual etiquette, supposing she were to say, straight out, "I'd like to go home alone tonight—but I'd really like to sleep with you tomorrow." Most men I know are nowhere near ready for the thought of a woman taking *that* lead. But in the brave new world, one hopes, sex won't have to be anybody's ego trip. In other words, she ought to have as much right as he to make a direct sexual "pass"—verbally or nonverbally—and he ought to be able to accept or reject it. And neither of them ought to get hung up about who goes first.

Watch your language

It is of course highly unlikely that Barbara Jordan, or any woman sophisticated enough to get elected to Congress, would be shocked by anything a congressman might say. In the recent past, women often thought they were liberated if they could not only keep from flinching at a man's obscenities but also outcuss him. Some feminists, on the other hand, have recently been citing a whole other reason for women to be offended by "dirty" words and "off-color" stories—at least those that relate to sexuality. Such words and stories, it is argued, are not shocking at all, but they *are* sexist, and thereby insulting to women. There is nothing in the least liberating about using phrases that reduce women (including oneself) to the four-letter sums of their sexual parts. Neither is it good dirty fun to swap jokes about dumb broads, big boobs, happy hookers or sex-starved old maids dreaming of rape. Sensitivity to sexual slurs has been rising, along with consciousness—just as it rose among blacks and other minority groups, to the point where the offended parties filed public protests. The public telling of racial jokes and the use of racial epithets has declined markedly in recent years. Women, the last permissible targets of slanderous humor, are finally learning not to smile politely any more. They stopped fainting long ago, and the redness in their faces now is not embarrassment—it's rage. In the new etiquette, sexist smut should be censored in polite society, just as racist smut is now. Not out of prudery, but simply because it has lost its power to amuse.

Guess who?

A woman with a professional title, sniffed the old social arbiters, forgoes it in the interest of convenience and social convention. Thus Dr. Joyce Brothers turns into Mrs. Milton Brothers after hours, and when Bernadette Devlin leaves Parliament, she is Mrs. McAlaskey, to you. In short, etiquette says that any woman whose name differs from her husband's, for professional reasons, or simply by choice, changes that name every time she's with him.

What's in a name, Romeo or no Romeo, is identity. And once a woman's social identity is merged with, or submerged in, her husband's, she tacitly submits to second-class personhood. That's etiquette as politics. And it's customs like this that are giving marriage a bad name.

The ultimate solution will probably be some system of combining last names, though a militant feminist may balk at keeping her "maiden" name—symbol as it is of her former status, which was to be identified through her father. Some couples even go so far as to adopt a brand-new surname that has no prior connection with either of them.

As I see it, this is the sort of area in which compromises will have to be made, unless we're all willing to take a number and let it go at that. Meanwhile the rule ought to be: Every woman for herself as long as nobody goes around calling anybody else's identity "socially inconvenient."

Members of the wedding (I do—or do I?)

Both Princess Anne and the unidentified American bride who wished to retain her own name offer living proof of the strange and well-nigh indestructible power of etiquette. However ludicrous a social convention becomes, the force of habit dies hard. And nowhere does it die harder than in the rituals of marriage, that bedrock of patriarchal society. The father still "gives" the bride away, as if she were chattel. Her veil and her white dress still signify chastity, despite the statistics on premarital sex. And the words of the service, "obey," "worship," "till death us do part," may provoke sly smiles, and in the case of well-known (or much-married) newlyweds, occasional tittering headlines, but nothing is done to make an honest woman of the bride. She is our last vestige of unliberated, role-playing femaleness.

Words, it is said, even the words of wedding vows, are only words. And people derive comfort from repeating them, especially in times of social upheaval. Comfort, yes, but false comfort. This is the kind of argument that confirms our worst suspicions about etiquette—that it is nothing but a snare and a delusion; a dainty tissue of lies and lip service. Poor Emily Post; that wasn't at all what she had in mind.

It is a hopeful sign that many young people have begun to rewrite the marriage service to suit the personal truths of their own relationships. Someday the official social arbiters, including the press, may liberate themselves from other hallowed—and hollow—traditions. Someday men's pictures will appear on the society pages along with women's. Laws will no longer require women to assume their husbands' names or domiciles.

Men will no longer be called heads of house. Who knows? Women may even feel free to handle cash in front of a waiter without striking terror in men's hearts.

Someday, finally, women will discover that the little courtesies they were taught to expect from men are too expensive a habit to maintain. As long as men are required to treat women as "ladies," women will have nothing but etiquette to show for a stunted life.

Anyway, I hope that in post–Emily Post society, we'll all consider it a hell of a way to pass seventh-grade biology.

Liberated women's pet peeves

1. Complimenting grown women by calling them "girls" (or "gals").

2. Referring to one's secretary as "my girl." (As in "I'll have my girl call yours and we'll set up a lunch date.")

3. At parties, tending the bar or the barbecue, but pointedly not sharing any other cooking, serving or clean-up chores.

4. Assuming the following remarks are complimentary:
(a) "You're much too cute to be an engineer [doctor, lawyer, Indian chief]!"
(b) "I understand you're an authoress!"—poetess, sculptress, lady doctor, jockette or any other term that implies the work is different when a woman does it. ("Actress" may be an exception, but only because the actor and the actress don't usually perform identical work. His profession is portraying men, while hers is portraying women. In almost all other cases, since the performer's gender has nothing whatever to do with what—or how well—she or he performs, there can be no reason for drawing the distinction except

obvious sexual bias. Does anybody think it's a coincidence that when stewardesses won pay equal to that of pursers, they were all officially renamed "flight attendants"?)

(c) "Hey, you think [play, drive, handle your job] just like a man!"

(d) "Hey, you think [play, drive, handle your job] pretty well for a girl!"

5. Offering assistance like this: "Let me help you with that, baby. A beautiful blonde [brunette, redhead] shouldn't struggle with a suitcase."

6. Referring affectionately to the woman in one's life as "my chick" or "my old lady," or, when married, "my better half."

7. Calling liberated women "women's libbers."

8. Not calling liberated women.

The Perfect Marriage

COOKING

The perfect wife does not tell her friends what a lousy cook her husband is.

The perfect husband does not tell his friends what a good cook his wife is.

CAREERS

The perfect wife doesn't object to her husband's having a career if it doesn't make him neglect his household duties.

The perfect husband doesn't object to his wife's *not* having a career if it doesn't make him neglect his household duties.

OPEN MARRIAGE

The perfect wife feels free to open the subject.
The perfect husband feels free to try closing it.

OTHER WOMEN

The perfect wife does not worry that if she stops being a perfect wife, other women will break up her marriage.

The perfect husband worries that if he stops being a perfect husband, other women will break up his marriage.

CHILDREN (SMALL)

For the perfect wife, small children are no problem. This is because where there are small children (including an imperfect husband), there is no such thing as a perfect wife.

CHILDREN (LARGE)

The perfect wife has stopped worrying about her daughter's having sex.

The perfect husband has stopped worrying about his son's having enough sex.

HOUSEWORK

The perfect wife does not nag the perfect husband about how dirty the house is. She installs light dimmers.

IDENTITY CRISIS

When a rude stranger asks, "What do *you* do?" the perfect husband does not cringe and mumble, "I'm just a homemaker."

The perfect wife strikes back with "How much do you make a year?"

HEAVY LIFTING

The perfect wife never says, "Oh, dear, I can't carry such a big load."

The perfect husband never says, "Make two trips."

CLOTHES

The perfect wife never complains about not having a thing to wear. She wears recycled patched denim, and when she and the perfect husband are dressing up to go out, *she's* ready first. (His hair takes longer.)

JEALOUSY

When either the perfect wife or the perfect husband finds strange blond hairs on the other's recycled patched denim, both understand that "jealousy" is a sick, destructive emotion caused by an archaic concept of marriage known as "sexual ownership." They are looking for a healthy, constructive emotion to replace "jealousy." Meanwhile they may have to give up strange blonds.

MENOPAUSE

The perfect wife won't tell jokes about his if he won't tell jokes about hers.

CONSCIOUSNESS-RAISING

The perfect wife comes home smiling from her weekly "C-R group" meeting. Two members of the group have left their husbands; two more are "into" adultery, and one refers to her spouse as "my attaché."

The perfect husband does not wait up for his wife. When she gets home, she finds him smiling, too—in his sleep.

LOOKS

The perfect wife does not need to be told she looks terrific for her age. She looks terrific, period, and she knows it.

The perfect husband knows she knows it.

SEX (MARITAL)

The perfect wife and the perfect husband know that when it comes to sex, no body's perfect.

SEX (EXTRAMARITAL)

See above.

LOVE

Love is never having to be (or be married to) a perfect wife.

Women Have Stopped Taking Dictation

"THIS SPRING, FASHION DICTATES . . ." REMEMBER THAT VOICE? IT had the ring of silken authority, if not naked truth. Occasionally it snapped "Off with your hat!" or "Down with your hem!" It told you when sequins were a must-have, and when they were a no-no; it said you would never look together without separates, or natural without false lashes. And best of all, it promised that you could be really something in a little black nothing.

Fashion's verbal wardrobe used to change every season, like the proverbial woman's mind. But the subliminal message was as timeless and clear-cut as a classic cashmere cardigan: "You are what you wear—and you wear what you're told."

Do women still tune in to that voice? Or is there ominous silence on the liberation front? Are the boutiques being evacuated? Have the walking wounded been cut down from their six-inch platform wedgies? Is everyone marching home from Bloomingdale's to embroider an upraised female fist on the seat of her boiled blue jeans?

In short, is it all over for clothes? If so, what are all those Ultrasuede people carrying in their crisp new shopping bags? Who is Halston and how come he's selling sweaters for $600? And why is a Watergate prosecutor wearing a mini-skirt in court?

The obvious answer is that it's far from over for clothes. But the somewhat less obvious answer is that Fashion is no longer dictating. Or, rather, that women have stopped taking dictation.

Many women still believe that you are what you wear. Chances are that, short of war, depression or a true social revolution that sheds blood as well as tradition, many women —and many men—will never cease to believe it.

And so what is happening has less to do with the importance of clothes in women's lives than with the importance of women's lives. The Cinderella era, in which every woman trusted in a magic ball gown to change her destiny, has finally struck midnight. People who wear glass slippers can't run for Congress.

Time was—and not all that long ago—you could go to a New York party and pick out the suburban matrons the minute they shrugged off their fun furs. Sometimes the minute *before.* You could tell something about a woman from the plunge of her neckline, or from the fact that she wore a lot of red, or that her jewelry sounded like an S-O-S. A serious career woman discreetly covered herself—and her success—with pastel knits lest anyone think she was pushy. Models deliberately tossed fluffy fox coats over their jeans, signifying that they were too busy to care that they were beautiful, excruciatingly thin, and earning $60 an hour.

Within the last year or two, a kind of fashion shorthand set in, so that you didn't even have to go to the party. Merely passing a woman in the street, you could "place" her. She defined herself for you by means of status badges—little gold

V's on her shoes, tiny Emilio's on her print dress, yellow fleurs-de-lis on her plastic bag. Check my labels, she telegraphed, and they will tell you who I am. Without the labels, who was she? The trouble was that even her hairdresser didn't know for sure. The symbols, the fashion signatures, had become a shorthand not only for her public but for the woman herself. They reassured her that she was a person of taste and knowledge. Someone who was with-it. Someone who wouldn't be caught dead without-it.

On the eve of liberation, there were millions of Cinderellas still trusting the spurious magic of Fashion. Millions of private-school girls, still hooked on the notion that in uniforms there is strength. Ah, the chic-anery of it. Even in Vermont communes, far from the ladies-who-lunch crowd, one had to slog through the mud in boots from L. L. Bean, *not* Abercrombie & Fitch.

Then there were the costume-party uniforms. Fashion told us to come as gauchos, as grannies, as go-go girls. Fashion decreed the see-through, which some of us saw through right away. But having emerged in the *après-midi* sun, we were finally talking back. From now on, some of us said, we'll come as we are.

A few who claimed to be truly liberated renounced dresses forever, along with cosmetics, and even clean hair. Maîtres d' at the classier restaurants bowed reluctantly to the pants suit. In Manhattan offices, receptionists took off the gloves and showed up for work in anything from Indian minis to dungarees. Functional clothing, they declared, for functioning persons.

Some of us had indeed come a long way. But not all in one direction. The fact remains that most of us—including the militant anti-fashion faction—are still "into" clothes, one way or another. Even a woman who wears torn jeans to work is using clothes to express something—probably anger at her boss, among other things. Chances are, if she got a raise and a promotion, she might even change her style.

So if Fashion is dead as a dictator, it is alive and well as a means of self-expression, of how we want others to see us, and of how we see ourselves.

Recently in my yoga class, a perfectly toned, size 8 leotard confided that she no longer owns a single dress. "I've decided skirts are strictly for mesomorphs," she explained, gliding into the lotus position. She thinks of clothes according to an esthetic physical standard. But she still thinks of clothes.

A single girl I know wears dirty jeans on dates with male chauvinists, as a matter of principle. With men she *likes,* she wears "stewardess" outfits—i.e., short-skirted and sexy. She is using clothes to play political games. But she is still using clothes.

A woman in my consciousness-raising group reluctantly gave up hot pants and mini-skirts when she realized that they clashed with her political image. "I liked the way my legs looked," she said, "but my legs are not where it's at." She wears (long) pants now, and occasionally a long party skirt. She won't carry a clutch bag, or wear high heels, or succumb to any clothing fad that restricts or hampers physical movement. But she looks attractive—and she *likes* looking attractive. She considers herself liberated—in her fashion. And she still buys clothes.

I even know a woman who has given up pants and gone back to loose, flowing skirts. She claims that pants (and pantyhose) are actually more restricting, and less healthy, for the female body. She considers herself liberated—in *her* fashion. And she, too, buys clothes.

Historically, women have not been the only ones enslaved by their mirror images. But except for Narcissus, men have always had other images as well—public identities quite apart from the reflected glory, or charm, bestowed by a Bill Blass blazer. Whereas until this point in time, as the fashionable phrase goes, it was a rare woman who could be sure that under her Dior, or her Saint Laurent, or her Alexander's line-for-line copy, there was a person of importance.

Some of us are just getting to know, and respect, that person. Some of us have just begun to raise our clothes-consciousness. Most of us are on the way to fashion liberation, which doesn't mean burning our clothes, but freeing ourselves to use and enjoy them as extensions of our individual selves. And then if we are what we wear, so be it.

How to Liberate Your Entire Family, in Your Own Home, Without Cost or Obligation

SOME PEOPLE'S HUSBANDS, I HEAR, ARE ALTOGETHER LIBERATED. They have gone so far as to sign, in *ink,* a marriage contract promising to love, honor and swab the children's bathroom every Thursday.

Other husbands, however, have been declared hopelessly unliberatable, by reason of advanced age (over forty? over *thirty*?), stiff-jointedness everywhere but around the tennis court and the persistent notion that a marriage contract means the bride comes with eight pigs and a donkey, so that if for any reason the husband is not completely satisfied, he may simply return the unused portion of the woman and keep the livestock, no questions asked. It goes without saying that under *this* marriage contract, there is no clause pertaining to the husband's having to swab anything whatsoever or even to hang up his shirt.

For the record, my husband stands, swaying slightly, about midpoint between these extremes. In other words, he cooks regularly but leaves the greasy pan unless yelled at. And while he regards me as an equal, a co-breadwinner, a *person,* the fact remains that when confronted by a grimy tile floor, he would never think of sinking to his knees with a bucket of suds and a sponge. Whereas *I* would never think of doing anything else.

I figure this moment of truth, or some variation thereof, has occurred over the last five years in approximately 82.4 percent of middle-class American marriages. According to my random, if not downright haphazard, sampling, one out of three of these couples claims to have solved the problem by employing a third person to handle the harsher realities of household life. That is, to do the swabbing. In my opinion, this does not count as a solution. It is a rank cop-out. Any wife who hires a maid is merely passing the bucket to another unliberated woman.

As for the other two out of three couples, my figures indicate that what they did was have a terrific fight about sharing the housework, after which he agreed to help, say, with the dishes, and she agreed not to bother him again about the dirt in the children's bathroom. In short, the women's movement has had virtually no effect on the practice of wife swabbing.

Note: In a few isolated cases, couples who are really hung up on the politics of housework have tried not cleaning the children's bathroom at all. This drastic experiment lasts an average of four days, at which point the wife sinks miserably to her knees with the bucket and sponge just as if nothing had happened. (It is a well-known fact that any husband resisting liberation is capable of withstanding the sight of his kids walking barefoot on a filthy tile floor. Indefinitely. This difference between the sexes is caused by something called cultural conditioning, for which no cure has yet been found.)

Anyway, on the basis of my exhaustive research, I have finally concluded that ours may be the only middle-class family in America to have taken the final revolutionary step toward total liberation. *Our children swab their own bathroom!* They also swab ours! Indeed, they vacuum the rugs, do the laundry and the grocery shopping, help prepare meals, do all cleaning up after meals, make their own beds, clean their rooms, dust, sweep and polish surfaces as needed and sew occasional buttons on their father's shirts. They are both boys, now in their teens; they were launched on this dazzling career when they were six and seven; and at this point I can honestly say that they run the house about as efficiently as the average bored housewife, give or take a few dust balls in the corners. Well, maybe not quite as efficiently. The average bored housewife feels guiltier about the dust balls in the corners. Tony and Roger do not have housewifely guilt going for them. All they have is parents who regularly check the corners and who operate under the following child-labor laws: (1) An hour or two of solid housework a day is a lot better for children than an hour or two of TV. (2) It is also better for their parents. (3) Ditto for the house.

And no, we don't pay our children money for any of this. Or rather, they get the same salary for housework as we do. Equal pay for equal work. Our position, as a family, is that we're all in this mess together. Tony and Roger—and Daddy—do not perform selected chores to "help Mommy." Because taking care of our house is not Mommy's job. It is the job of everyone who lives in the house.

My husband, who is a psychiatrist specializing in treating adolescents, believes that in most troubled homes the trouble never started with "permissiveness." It started with the lack of any real family interaction. A house in which Mommy mostly works, Daddy mostly relaxes and the kids mostly play is not a healthy environment for any of them. In our house everyone has to work part time. We may never be spotless, but we're livable. And more important, we work as a team.

I have a friend named Sue who spends her days aimlessly picking up after her husband and two able-bodied children, eight and ten. As she wanders forlornly through the wreckage of their rooms, wiping and complaining, her daughter, Lisa, sits nearby making yet another mess.

Then there's my other friend, Nancy, an artist who has three children, ages six to thirteen. "I *tell* them to make their beds," wails Nancy. "But they *refuse.*" "You make my bed, Mommy," one said. "You don't have anything important to do."

Never mind that her mommy is a professional painter whose work has hung in museums. The six-year-old believes that housework is Mommy's "real" job and knows that Mommy will always give in anyway.

Have you ever noticed what happens the first time a mother like this visits her child in summer camp? "That can't be *my* Johnny's bed!" she cries, noting the perfect hospital corners. And where are Johnny's clothes? All folded neatly in his trunk? Impossible! She stares at Johnny's counselor in stunned disbelief. The entire bunk is immaculate. Not a dust ball, not a cobweb, not a pair of dirty socks in sight. At home Johnny is an utter nine-year-old slob. So are all his bunkmates. How come there are no nine-year-old slobs in summer camp? *I* know how come. Because in camp there are *no mothers to do the housework.* When young children *have* to be homemakers, they can be the best in the business. Think about it.

There are lots of jobs a child can just naturally do better than any grownup. Being built closer to the floor, they can dust the baseboards in half the time. They bend more easily. They don't get backaches. They also take better to tedious small jobs, like slicing vegetables, cleaning shrimp, sorting clothes, polishing doorknobs. And they get a positive charge out of running major appliances. Pushing buttons to activate a dishwasher, being in control of a sophisticated vacuum cleaner—you can't hardly give a twentieth-century child a greater sense of power, short of letting her drive your car on the freeway.

The simple fact is that most kids can do more than most

parents think they can. But unless they really have to, they won't.

Like most revolutionary new ideas, our family's "system" is neither new nor revolutionary, which is probably for the best. We find that when a startled visitor clucks sympathetically about "poor little Roger" having to fold underwear in the laundry room before he can go out and play dodge ball, it is better to cite solid historical precedents than to mumble catchy slogans about women's lib.

A hundred years ago in rural America, for instance, every child was looked on first as an extra mouth to feed, and then —as soon as possible—as another pair of hands to help run the farm. The minute that little pair of hands grew dexterous enough to hold chicken feed, the kid was up at 5 A.M. feeding chickens. I doubt if any child in those good (hard) old days ever felt useless, alienated, bored or powerless. The family really *needed* every one of its children, and the children knew it.

Nobody *needs* children now, except possibly mothers who would feel useless, alienated, bored or powerless without their clinging to her. Like the woman on my block whose life is dedicated to the relentless force-feeding of her two grossly overweight youngsters. She stuffs them as if they were Alsatian geese destined for the *foie gras* market. "They are my whole life!" she explains. "Gee," I murmured to her once. "That's too bad."

According to Parkinson's Law, work expands to fill the time available. But women—especially mothers—have adopted this principle with a vengeance. I can still remember my husband patiently teaching Roger at the age of four to tie his shoelaces. He was the first child in his nursery-school class to master this feat. Yet I know at least three mothers who are still tying laces for eight-year-olds. Is it because those children really can't function by themselves? Or because their mothers are afraid to find out they can?

We live in New York City, and our children walk fifteen blocks to and from school. Unlike suburban children, they can also travel alone—usually on foot—to museums, parks, after-school dates at friends' houses and the dentist's office.

But my friend Doris, whose children are the same age as ours, refuses to let them go anywhere without her. Doris' life is a constant whirl of taxi and bus rides, fetching and ferrying Joanie or David to and from judo class, birthday parties, piano lessons and skating rinks. I called her one morning during a violent thunderstorm and she said, "I can't talk now—I have to get to David's school by eleven-forty." David had forgotten his lunch box.

"It's pouring out!" I said. "Somebody's bound to give him half a sandwich. He won't *starve,* for heaven's sake."

Doris was shocked. She wouldn't dream of not tearing across town in the rain with that lunch box. "David would never forgive me," she said. *Seriously.*

I know another harassed woman who teaches part-time and gets overwhelmed with household errands. She claims her nine-year-old can't be "trusted" even to go to the store. "He'd come back with fifteen dollars' worth of chocolate cookies!" she says. I have heard women say the same thing about their husbands. "He'd only buy stuffed anchovies. He's no help at all."

They must be joking, mustn't they? But unfortunately they mean every word.

Tony and Roger do about two thirds of our supermarketing. If they make a mistake—buy the wrong kind of lettuce, get the wrong change, forget the milk—they get sent back until it's right. We expect them to shop carefully—pick each tomato, not buy three in a cellophane box. They are also expected to check weights, compare prices, examine the eggs for cracks, read ingredient labels.

I think they enjoy being sensible consumers. They may even eat more sensibly than many kids their age.

Of course, there are a fair number of jobs they don't enjoy. Just like grownups. But I could never see the point of pretending that running a home is all good clean fun. Frying bacon is more pleasant than scouring a greasy griddle, but one doesn't go without the other and they may as well know it now.

Nothing irritates me more than a television commercial showing a perfectly groomed woman smiling inanely over her scouring pad. Whom is she kidding? Not me. And certainly not Tony or Roger.

I readily confess that the system isn't foolproof. We've had whole spinach soufflés dropped on the floor. We've had dirt swept under rugs, or not swept at all. Wool sweaters have been fatally shrunk in the dryer at high heat.

Some women might argue that it's easier to do it oneself, after all, if the alternative is yelling yourself hoarse to ensure that the kids do it right. I disagree. In the first place, I can yell effectively from the depths of a comfy sofa or even from behind a clacking typewriter in my upstairs office. Second, yelling is kinder to my hands than the gentlest detergent. And third, my husband willingly shares at least half the yelling chores. (He does a superb job, too.)

So on balance, we think we've got a pretty good thing going. The children are learning to take care of themselves and of the things that make up their life and ours. They are learning that sharing, and meaningful work, are an important part of what a family is all about. And in the process they are learning that there is no such thing as "woman's" work, or "man's," or "child's." They are just as proud that they can sew on a button as they are of learning to sail a boat. And *we* are just as proud.

We're also aware that the romance isn't going to last forever. When he was eight, Tony used to love making the salad at dinnertime. Being entrusted with a sharp knife was enormously exciting, and he took an artist's pride in the finished product. Somehow, at twelve the thrill was gone. Any housewife would recognize the symptom. After you've sliced your 600th scallion, the old magic just isn't there any more. With a child, it may only take 300 scallions. What happens is, they get sloppy. Sloppi*er*. They complain more, have more accidents, "forget" how it's supposed to be done.

When we reach the point of diminishing returns—and we will—it will be time for still another revolutionary step. And I already know what it is: a massive child-exchange program, in which young teen-agers would leave home for a year or two and work—for pay—with other people's families. The principle, again, is not really new. Kids used to serve apprenticeships. Later they took up baby-sitting or working as mother's helpers. They have always walked neighbors' dogs, mowed neighbors' lawns, shoveled snow off neighbors' driveways. And again, they've always been better at the same jobs when performing them away from home.

As I see it, this concept ought to be applied on a national scale. Two years' service in a Family Corps instead of military conscription. Boys and girls both. They could travel to another part of the country, to live and work with another kind of family—again adding to their growth, development and knowledge of life. Midway in the teen years, that critical, impossible phase when the young are so torn between the continuing need for security and adult guidance and the emerging need to break out from under their parents' thumbs —a Family Corps could really be the answer. It would provide a continuing secure family situation—yet one that would also be recognized as a responsible, paying job. A job, what's more, that almost any youngster could handle beautifully— assuming that, like Tony and Roger, he or she had eight to ten years of basic training at home.

As for the new family to which such a boy or girl would be assigned, where could they find a better solution to *their* household-help problem? Wanted: Bright, energetic, experienced young homemaker who can cook, clean and help run a family—his parents', yours or mine, and someday, his or her own.

That's what I call total liberation.

P.S. Once upon a time I read Tony and Roger a news item about Richard Nixon and an unidentified eleven-year-old girl. Nixon was greeting a crowd of New Yorkers when the little girl grasped his hand and said earnestly that she hoped to go into politics too when she grew up. The then-President smiled and said, "Oh, you're much too pretty. You'll probably get married and have a family."

I read the story to my children in a neutral tone, hoping for maybe an "Ugh" of disgust by way of response. (Feminist parents are always hoping for encouraging "Ughs" from their liberated children.) But when I finished reading, Tony and Roger looked nonplused. "Boy, that's *weird*!" Roger exclaimed. "Yeah," Tony agreed. "Weird."

"Why?" I asked.

"Well," said Roger, *"Nixon'*s married, isn't he?"

That was when I realized we must be doing something right.

Guess Who's Not Coming to Dinner

IT IS WHISPERED IN THE TOWN THAT SOME PERSONS HAVE LIBERated themselves from the custom of entertaining each other. When invited out, they phone in their regrets promptly, without murmuring about rain checks or some-other-times. They refrain from incurring social obligations through careless remarks such as "Say, why don't we have the Beasleys over? Tom Beasley goes wild over your molasses nut drops."

I know one couple who, when asked to parties, go so far as to accept—after announcing cheerfully, "You understand, we *never* reciprocate." This couple doesn't get around much any more. But then, as they see it, solitary confinement means never having to give a party.

Our friends Tom and Didi always say, "We've got to get together next week," but when it comes to the delicate question "Our place or yours?" Tom and Didi remain tellingly silent. We don't see much of them, actually, except when we run into each other at someone else's Open House.

As for Doria, the feminist activist, she confesses that every so often she still has "people in," but that when she does, it involves a serious attack of partyphobia, with all the classic symptoms: glazed eyes from reading recipes for nutmeat-stuffed gherkins and mock duck; the empty-cart syndrome (wandering up and down supermarket aisles, snatching recklessly at gourmet canned goods), and, finally, the "overdrawn" feeling caused by caterer's bills or the serving of crabmeat cornucopias and smothered squab to twenty dieters, picky eaters and ovo-lacto-vegetarians. Doria last had "people in" about a year ago. She is thinking of trying again soon, but not very.

Once upon a time I tried to "entertain" too. Casually, like it says in the magazines. A few friends, a simple buffet dinner, clean napkins and snappy conversation. For two weeks beforehand I would lie awake nights counting tidbits-in-blankets and worrying about the (Raspberry) Bombe. Days I spent selecting dangerous ingredients in exotic markets—ingredients I knew perfectly well would explode when mixed. Thin-skinned oranges of even size. Phosphate baking powder. Elderberry blossoms. The menu was revised and edited more times than the lead paragraph of a 700-page historical sex novel. Would the Tipsy Torte be too rich, after the pickled-lamb-tongue salad? Would the Pineapple Upside-Down Cake come out Rightside-Up? Was herring out of season in a month without a P in it?

Then there was the problem of execution. To wit: How could one heat the cranberry fingers at 375 degrees, when the turnip cups needed 450, and the corn zephyrs 475? Should one pop the zephyrs into a neighbor's oven? Would one then have to invite the neighbor? What about the neighbor's roommate, who is known to be allergic to pickled tongue?

When I "entertained," I always ended up serving a surprise. Not a tomato surprise, just a surprise. There was no telling whether anyone would eat it. Sometimes they did, which surprised me.

When I "entertained," I celebrated quietly in the kitchen, spattered with piquant sauce to match the wallpaper. I would hover there anxiously, somewhere between the crusted casseroles and the other burnt offerings. Macédoines and dull knives would litter the available counter space until some thoughtful guest would bring out the greasy serving platters and pile them neatly on top of the dessert.

When I "entertained," I could always faintly hear the guests laughing in another room. I would thank heaven they were amused, which meant they hadn't noticed how long I'd been out of the room, fumbling. Unless of course that was what amused them.

When I "entertained," I would drink too much wine and laugh high, terrified laughter. I would choke on my own coffee and spill on my own sofa, murmuring reassuringly, "Oh, it's nothing, nothing at all."

I desperately wanted to say all the bright, modest things one says at one's own successful parties. Deft, knowing little phrases like "Thank you," and "Oh, these? I just caramelized them in ramekins." All said lightly, with dry hand gestures and tinkling ice cubes.

Instead I would lower my eyes to the tarnished cake knife and the wet rings where there weren't any coasters, and the flowing ashtrays which I had meant to empty before dinner, only the corn zephyrs were burning in my next-door neighbor's oven.

When I "entertained," I did not have a lovely time, thank you.

I don't know whether the giving *up* of party-giving is a trend, or just a phase we'll all outgrow when everyone is well and truly liberated, and only the caterer rolls in dough. But sometimes I imagine a society where there is *no entertaining* at all. People live in caves, stirring their private stews in crude pots, over crude fires. And when a friendly passer-by passes by, the stirrer within lifts his ladle and grunts, "Hey, taste this and tell me if it needs another pinch of batwing fuzz!"

In my dream, the passer-by takes a sip and grunts back, "Hey! Sure wish the stirrer in my cave could make a crude batwing stew taste like this."

"Well," says the genial stirrer, "why don't you both drop in later and have a fistful with us? Seven-thirtyish?"

"On one condition," grunts the passer-by, who has a sense of history about him.

"What's that?" grunts the stirrer.

"Not a word of this ever goes beyond this room."

The ERA Account

HILDY AND I HAVE FINALLY FIGURED OUT WHAT TO DO ABOUT THE Equal Rights Amendment; we only hope it's not too late. Either way, though, Hildy still plans to finish her book about ERA. She can just change the title from "ERA! How We Got It Passed" to "ERA? We Almost Got It Passed, But . . ."

Hildy is, of course, in the "creative" advertising game. She's handled the campaigns for all sorts of new improved stuff that women don't really think they need until Hildy leans on them a little. Most of her accounts have been for products that ought to be a lot trickier to sell than a soft, naturally fragrant, equal right. She's sold form-fitting room fresheners in decorator colors. Slow-talking cereal for kids with learning disabilities. No-fault dishwasher detergent. In all her years on Madison Avenue, I can think of only one certified flop that Hildy ever had. It was a game called On Your Own, which combined the worst features of solitaire and Monopoly, so middle-aged women could play it on nights their husbands forgot to come home from the office.

When Hildy called me in as an ERA consultant, or "amendment doctor," I told her I didn't know beans about law or advertising. She said that was no problem, as long as I knew something about kids. She thinks kids are just the angle we need to put ERA over the top.

"Kids?" I asked her. "Why kids?"

"Because," she explained patiently, "ERA is really for kids. Never should have been pitched to grownups in the first place." We ought to switch gears immediately, she said, get the President and Mrs. Carter off the phone with the state senators—and put Amy on instead.

The minute she said that, I knew she was on to something. Little girls! How come nobody had thought of it? If ERA passes, who's got the most to gain and the least to lose? You guessed it. Besides, if an equal right will make a little girl happy ("Aw, please, Daddy, we can afford it, can't we?"), what kind of Daddy would say no? Surely not a state senator.

Already I could hear myself humming a few bars from the new hit single, "I'm Gonna Do Equal Right By My Baby," recorded by Engelbert Humperdinck and the Rolling Stones. Hildy smiled indulgently.

"Do the ERA people know how big little girls are this year?" I bubbled excitedly. "I mean, do they know how every new star in Hollywood is fourteen or under? Look at the tennis champs and gymnasts! How about right here on Broadway? How old is the newest leading lady? Thirteen—with an entire chorus line that ranges downward from twelve to seven!"

"If they knew all that," said Hildy wryly, "they wouldn't need us." She tossed her memo pad at me and started pacing. "Now then," she barked, "we've got to write some thirty-second TV spots. Sure-fire stuff. Hard sell. Wall-to-wall kids for ERA—preferably in tears. You can do the one for that new pigtailed tennis whiz, Tracy Austin. And work in a cameo bit for Nadia Comaneci—she could tell Tracy why Rumanian girl gymnasts don't defect to the U.S."

"Got it," I said. "Tracy and Nadia are standing forlornly outside this junior high school yard—noses pressed against the wire fence. Locked out. Inside the fence, boys in federally funded warm-up suits practice flexing medals and trophies. Close-up of the big sign that says NO GIRLS. Then we get the voice-over male principal, explaining that in this school, boys still get exclusive use of the play yard—plus the gym—during recess. 'Boys need the exercise, you know.' "

"Not bad," said Hildy, scribbling notes. "But try one for Jodie Foster. Or Tatum O'Neal."

"Hmm," I mused, "Jodie and Tatum are sitting forlornly on a bench outside this film-making workshop. Inside, boys are yelling 'Roll 'em!' and 'Take three!' The voice-over principal explains that in this school, boys can take film or photography shop, or electronics, or metal, woodworking . . . but girls may choose cooking, sewing or embroidery. Period.

"Jodie looks up tearfully. 'Please, sir,' she asks, 'what do we do in embroidery shop?'

"The principal replies crisply, 'Learn to decorate a beanie.' "

Hildy nodded. "Possible," she said. "But maybe we'll just go with a punchy ten-second spot for Amy Carter."

"Let's see. Amy's all alone in her new treehouse, drowning her sorrows in five-cent lemonade. The voice-over principal asks why she's crying. And Amy sobs, 'Daddy says I can't have equal rights—even if I grow up to be President.' "

Hildy thought we were off to a pretty good start, but she was still worried about one thing: should we change the name of the amendment—to something less scary?

"What's scary about equal rights?" I asked her.

Hildy shrugged. "What was scary about cake mixes?"

I confessed I didn't get the connection. Cake mixes, Hildy explained, were the classic case of a good, maybe terrific, idea whose time had come—and whose promoters were stunned to discover that women wouldn't buy it. Madison Avenue spent a fortune before they found out what went wrong.

"Housewives weren't as lazy as other people?"

"Of course they were," snapped Hildy.

"Families didn't love moist, velvety cake?"

"Of course they did," snapped Hildy again.

"Well, then, what?"

Scary," said Hildy. "Moist, velvety cake that jumped right out of a box meant that nobody needed Mom in the kitchen any more. It wasn't just calling her lazy. It was calling her obsolete."

"Hmm," I said thoughtfully. "How did they ever fix that?"

"Repackaging. They left out an essential ingredient—so Mom would feel everybody still needed her. They said, 'You add your own fresh eggs!' And she did. That was it—pure genius. They liberated the American home-baker—and she didn't even notice!"

I had always wanted to say "Eureka," and here was my chance. "Eureka," I said. "ERA still hasn't come up with the political equivalent of an eggless cake mix!"

"Exactly," said Hildy. "And meanwhile, look at what the anti-ERA women are up to." She pulled out a recent news photo of women in frilly aprons marching on the Florida statehouse, with signs saying "Don't Equalize Me" in one hand, and a homemade cake or pie in the other.

"Okay," I said. "First we rename the amendment. We call it AYOFE instead of ERA. Then we get all our kids, wearing chef's hats, to march on statehouses yelling, "We want AYOFE! We want AYOFE!"

"AYOFE?" muttered Hildy doubtfully.

"Sure. The Add Your Own Fresh Eggs Amendment."

Hildy shook her head.

"What's wrong with it?" I said.

"It'll never sell in Peoria."

Leading Ladies

IT WAS THE NIGHT THEY BROUGHT US THE MRS. AMERICA PAGEANT live from Las Vegas that the topic of First Ladies came up. For all I know, the topic of First Ladies comes up every year on the night of the Mrs. America pageant, and we just never noticed.

Anyhow, everyone at this dinner party was startled when the political scientist in the rumpled tweed suit suddenly said, "First Ladies are *phfft.*"

In Las Vegas it had just been announced that the fifty Mrs. America contestants were asked, "Who is the woman you most admire in the whole world?" and 73 percent of them had failed to name a First Lady. For perhaps the first time in the history of that question, "Mamie Eisenhower" was not the answer.

"*Phfft?* That's a vile thing to say," a woman in intense orange pajamas snapped at the political scientist. "First Ladies are both useful and charming. All the world loves a First Lady."

"That's true," said a young TV executive in aviator glasses. "They love Mrs. Israel, because she kept her mad money stashed in a Washington, D.C., bank. Which cost her husband his job."

Someone giggled. "And they love Mrs. Canada, because she ran away from home to become a rock groupie. Which may cost *her* husband his job."

"She's not a rock groupie," Orange Pajamas retorted indignantly. "She's an aspiring photojournalist."

"That's a rock groupie with a magazine assignment," explained the political scientist.

In Las Vegas they were asking the semifinalists what they remembered best about their wedding day. Mrs. South Dakota, I think it was, remembered her husband's face. "It was so . . . *clean,*" she murmured.

"Seriously," said the political scientist. "Look at what's happening to First Ladies. They are *all* having an identity crisis."

"Mmm," mused Aviator Glasses. "Mrs. Argentina thought for a minute she was president. And Mrs. China thought for a minute she was chairman—"

"—and Mrs. Ford thought for a minute she was entitled to her opinion," sighed the hostess, boldly adding two saccharin tablets to her coffee. "Do you think that cost her husband *his* job?"

"Who knows?" sighed a shy first novelist in a flamboyant gypsy costume. "But at least they got his-and-hers book contracts. Which was more than any previous First Lady ever got for just smiling nicely."

"Do you think it was *easy* being a First Lady who just smiled nicely?" said Aviator Glasses. "Think of the trouble Caesar's wife had just being above suspicion."

In Las Vegas a minister's wife in a swimsuit was explaining what her husband would do if she was wearing a very sexy dress at a party, and other men were expressing interest. "He'd enjoy it," she said serenely, with a smile that could only be described as First Ladylike. "Because *he knows I'm all his.*"

"Now, there's a wife," said Aviator Glasses, "who'd be an asset to any *Playboy* interview."

"How do you think Imelda Marcos—Mrs. Philippines—would have answered that?" mused Orange Pajamas.

"Imelda Marcos," said the political scientist dourly, "would have referred the question to her husband, who is said to be a political power in his own right."

The hostess was saying she thought recent First Ladies had suffered from overspecialization. She noted, for instance, that Mrs. Johnson had to major in "Beautification," because Mrs. Kennedy had taken culture, interior design and conversational French. Someone observed that Rosalynn Carter hasn't picked her major yet, but that whatever it is, it will be something Eleanor Roosevelt would have approved of.

Nobody could remember Mrs. Nixon's specialty and everyone agreed that Betty Ford had really just dabbled in being outspoken.

"Republican First Ladies," Orange Pajamas said, "don't have to take an interest. Unless they want a book contract."

"Well," said the political scientist, "Mamie had bangs. At the time it seemed more than enough."

The gypsy novelist said she had once met a First Lady from an emerging nation. "She had this photo album with three hundred and seventy-two color portraits of herself standing on a lawn next to various world leaders. Presidents, prime ministers, oil sheiks, military-industrial complexes . . ."

"Was she happy?" asked Orange Pajamas.

"Miserable," said the novelist. "There were only two things in life she wanted to do, and she couldn't do either of them."

"What things?" asked the political scientist, stifling a yawn.

"Go to the beach all by herself, and find someone she could talk to about Harry Belafonte."

In Las Vegas a Mrs. America finalist in evening gown was wrestling with her last fateful question: "What would your husband do if you decided to run for President of the United States?" There was an audible hush on the TV proceedings, and even at the party everyone but the political scientist fell strangely silent. After all, a black mink, a microwave oven, a trip to Europe, a Toyota and an entire wardrobe of sheer pantyhose were riding on the woman's answer.

"He would . . ." she hesitated. And smiled.

"Oh, *don't* say he'd lose his job!" gasped Aviator Glasses.

"Ssh, for God's sake!" exclaimed Orange Pajamas. "She's *thinking.*"

The contestant drew a deep, assertive breath. "He'd . . . be my campaign manager!"

Everyone at the party applauded, except the political scientist, who groaned. But they loved it in Las Vegas. In fact, she won.

Just before the party broke up, some of the guests collaborated on a list of suggested test questions for the judges to spring on next year's Mrs. America contestants. From among more than two hundred lovely and talented entries, these were selected on the basis of charm, intelligence, poise, personality, accomplishment, outside interests and, of course, beauty.

1. If you opened an illegal $20,000 bank account, would you show your husband the free hot tray, golf clubs, Corning cookware and digital clock-radio you got?

2. If you knew that your husband sometimes lusted in his heart, would you let him pick the books for your nine-year-old daughter to read at the dinner table?

3. If you were a First Lady, who would be the rock star you most admired in the whole world?

4. Would you prefer your husband to be refreshingly outspoken, or to take a special interest in, say, photography?

5. Do you think First Ladies are *phfft*?

Trading Up

WHEN I FIRST MET GLINDA, SHE WAS A CUSTOMER'S WOMAN ON Wall Street. That was shortly before she went into designing sheets, dishes and small leather goods. We lost track for a time, during which I heard she had either opened a seafood restaurant or become a sex therapist, or both.

Maggie used to write murder mysteries, seated on a bench in Carl Schurz playground, while her children quietly poured sand over mine. Maggie is in New Mexico now, running for Congress.

Meanwhile, Sue-Ellen the math teacher has started operating a health club; Lenore the health-club operator has started teaching math, and my old friend Abigail, the writer and editor, is going off to law school.

I suppose I should have spotted the trend before Anita Bryant, a runner-up Miss America who used to sing for her orange juice, suddenly launched an alarming overnight career in professional homophobia.

Anyway, I suspect I am the last woman on my block who

isn't, for good or ill, embarking on a new life's work. I am not talking about a mere job change, of course, or even about developing a new skill in the same general area—like a painter who leaves a blue period and enters a green one, or a feisty actress who takes over her movie studio. What I am referring to is what, in the plumbing-supply field, would be called a complete retooling.

Everybody knows the women's movement has lured millions of career homemakers back into the job market, or into school, to finish preparing for careers that were dumped in favor of family life. But this newer phenomenon—perfectly good, sound, successful careers being dumped, at age thirty-five, in favor of starting over at the bottom of a whole other ladder—is a résumé entry of a different color.

It started out as a spotty fad, something like barefoot weddings with matching contracts about who gets to empty the cat litter on alternate Thursdays. Any minute I expected to hear of at least one stolid woman banker abandoning her bourgeois spouse to go paint golden, lush-bodied youths on a South Sea island.

But career-swapping seems to be a good deal more complicated than that. Putting aside mere boredom as a motivation (on the ground that it is merely boring), I think I'm beginning to see why women, even more than men, are doing it—and why it's a good thing they are.

In the first place, today's thirty-five-year-old woman may be the last of her sex who never had to decide, at the age of ten, what she wanted to be when she grew up. In the mid-fifties, when that question was put to her, today's thirty-five-year-old woman smiled and said "a mommy." If she smiled and said anything else—say, "owner of a seafood restaurant," "congressperson from New Mexico," "elderly Peace Corps volunteer" or "oil baron"—the grownup who had asked her chuckled nervously, and set her straight.

Come to think of it, I once met a boy whose reply to that

momentous question, at age ten, elicited the same set of nervous chuckles and hasty straight-settings from his disapproving elders. I remember giggling when he complained about it; I simply didn't believe him. After all, it used to be a well-known fact that boys could say they wanted to grow up to be absolutely anything, within reason. "What," I asked him, "did you say you wanted to be?" And he replied solemnly, "A mommy."

These days his fantasy may not seem all that weird to some front-line feminists, but I daresay his Uncle Lou would still prefer it if he stuck to "oil baron"—or better yet, "a dentist like Uncle Lou."

In any case, it delights me (except in the case of Anita Bryant) that so many successful career women are suddenly leaping forward into great productive unknowns, many of them taking serious financial risks to do it, and all of them making wrenching changes in everything from their love life to their children's TV-cartoon habits.

Back in the old days—like 1970—I didn't know a woman who would disrupt a working life style for anything, unless she had to. Divorce, widowhood, financial ruin, husband's transfer to Keokuk might befall her—and occasionally force her to plunge headlong into a decent, satisfying new kind of work. When it did, everyone thought that the woman was lucky, and also set for life. Back in the old days, nobody—not even she—ever wondered what she might want to do after she survived.

But now there are women like my friend Abigail, who has been surviving nicely for quite a few years and is about to quit her swell job, doing something she did very well and liked very much, in order to try something harder. Not more "creative." Not more "fulfilling." *Harder.* Because trying something harder means never having to say you're settling.

I asked Abigail the other day what a nice girl like her was doing in a mid-life career change. And she smiled. "I decided

I'd like to become a Supreme Court Justice instead."

"Then it's power you're after?" I suggested.

She shrugged. "Possibly. Though I think power may be overrated, like fame. Not that either of them isn't nice—they are. I just don't believe in them as goals. They're really just fringe benefits, like tenure and the flowing black robe. Anyway, I don't think I understand power. Autonomy I understand."

We discussed Elizabeth Janeway's definition of power: "the ability not to have to please." Abigail remembered reading that a few years ago and repeating it excitedly to all her friends—until a male friend said that it wasn't what power was at all. "He said it was 'the ability to make things happen,' " Abigail recalled. "And I thanked him. Now I had a full set of power definitions—his and hers."

If she gets to be a Supreme Court Justice, I reminded her, it'll be male-definition power she has. "Hmm," she said, "well, that's okay. But it's not why I want to be there."

"Why, then?"

She smiled again. "Because that's where the law gets most interesting. And I figure if I'm going to influence the law at all, why not do it where it counts the most?"

I couldn't think of a good reason why not.

The other important thing about Abigail is that she always knew she was smart. But in the last two years she's discovered that she's *very* smart. All her life she has also been pretty, charming and funny. Which meant that, until now, she's never had to use all the smartness. She's never had to explore it, stretch it or lean on it to get where she wanted to go. Abigail assumes that one doesn't need looks, charm and personality to get to the Supreme Court. She may even be right.

Before I left her I asked her two children, Edward, eleven, and Margaret Rose, eight, what they wanted their mother to be when she grows up. Here's what they said:

Edward: "I think law will be nice for her. I was a little

worried at first, but I've had a change of heart. I changed my mind about what I want to be too. I used to want to be a cryptanalyst. But now I'm considering computer programming."

Margaret Rose: "A writer was terrific. If she's a lawyer, she may not get so famous. Which means I may not get my name in the paper so much, which I love.

"On the other hand, if she's a lawyer, maybe she'll go more places and take me, which I love. And if being a lawyer is too hard, she can always go back and be a writer. Can't she?"

I said I thought my friend Abigail could do anything. Which Margaret Rose loved.

All Hair the Conquering Heroine

KIMBERLEY ANN, NINE, HAS JUST DECIDED WHAT SHE WANTS TO BE when she grows up: a part-time cocktail waitress with frosted blond streaks. It is probably just a coincidence that Kimberley Ann's mother recently graduated from law school and lopped off her two-tone gold ringlets right at the dark roots.

Kim's classmate Janice, who is still eight, has her heart set on becoming a file clerk who ties up her hair in a severe bun that can be shaken free, with a single lightning stroke, into a quivering mass of raven tendrils. (Janice's mother is a securities analyst, with a naturally frizzled pepper-and-salt pageboy.)

Nina, ten and a half, plans to be a schoolteacher with a firm grip and frosted blond highlights. And twelve-year-old Stephanie, the cynic, intends to become a frosted blond highlight, period.

Clearly, a fair number of feminists' daughters are having "role model" trouble. The cause seems to be a sudden and widespread cultural confusion about the difference—if any—between a role model and a hair model. As I understand it, a role model is an adult person of your own gender whom you admire and want to be like: a President, an astronaut, a nuclear physicist, a private eye. Whereas a hair model is a stunning, raven-haired President; a luscious redheaded astronaut; a blond bombshell of a nuclear physicist; a frost-streaked poster pinup of a private eye.

It would be easy to blame the confusion on television's newest rage—the female "action-adventure" star who can either ride a motorcycle, toe-tap on a skateboard, shoot straight, do heavy lifting or figure out how to trap a criminal while wearing a dripping wet Bunny costume. After all, no matter what else these new wonder women do besides wonders—and part-time file-clerking, schoolteaching, cocktail-waitressing—the thing they all do *best* is their hair.

So it would be easy to blame TV, but, as one of our stunning raven-haired ex-Presidents used to say, "it would be wrong." The truth is, we have always had a little trouble spotting the subtle line between a heroine and a hairdo. In a highly unscientific recent survey, mothers of nine- to twelve-year-olds, selected solely on the basis of shampoo, color tint and permanent-wave length, were asked the following question: When you were between nine and twelve, who was your "role model," and why?

• Seventeen percent answered "Esther Williams, the swimming star, because she could do fifteen minutes of flawless underwater sidestroke with gorgeous flowers twined in her braided coronet."

• Twenty-five percent named Brenda Starr, the comic-strip girl reporter, on the basis of her sensational headline set in bold-type curls the color of "a five-alarm fire," an "Irish setter" or a *"saumon fumé."*

• Twelve percent had idolized Sonja Henie, the Goldilocks of the ice, because she skated like a wind-up Christmas angel; her hair and feet set off "matching sparks of white light"; she was an "animated gold sequin."

• The remainder chose a wide assortment of heroines ranging

from the Dragon Lady (dangerous mastermind set in a black curtain of silk hair) to Amelia Earhart and Dale, Flash Gordon's dauntless co-pilot, both of whom had their heads in clouds of wispy gold tendrils escaping from under their flying helmets.

Nobody had a role model with nonterrific hair.

Film historian Molly Haskell has noted that the long, sexy tresses of movie queens in the hard-boiled dramas of the 1940s was the female equivalent of a gun—an ultimate woman's weapon in a tough man's world of crime and carnality. The new "action" heroines of the seventies, operating in the same man's world, actually get to wield both weapons—the hair *and* the gun. But it's the same old game: Everything, including the girls, is still owned and operated by the fellow who runs the beauty parlor. Body, soul, gun and frost job, they are strictly *Charlie's* angels.

Armed with this valuable knowledge, I recently watched my first episode of the TV series *Charlie's Angels,* accompanied by two hard-core nine-year-old fans, Nicole and Sandy. Here's how it went:

ME: Tell me about the "angels."

NICOLE: Well, first off you have to know which is which. Sabrina is the smart one, Kelly is strong, and Jill is beautiful. Mostly her hair.

ME: But they're *all* beautiful.

SANDY (patiently): Of *course.* But Sabrina is beautiful *and* smart. Kelly is beautiful *and* strong. Jill is *just* beautiful. Mostly her hair.

ME: Oh. (On the screen, three women are flashing guns, hair, sexy clothes and dazzling smiles, like armed stewardesses serving plastic filet mignon. (Pause.) Which would you rather be—the smart one, the strong one, or the beautiful one, with the hair?

NICOLE: Definitely not the beautiful one.

SANDY: Obviously.

ME: Why obviously?

NICOLE: Because even if she has the most hair, she has the smallest part. (Sandy nods solemnly.)

ME: What if you had a choice, I mean in real life? You could be smart and strong—or you could be beautiful. Which would you choose?

SANDY: Why couldn't we be all three?

ME: Well, first off, because hardly anybody gets to be all three. And hardly anybody even gets to have a choice. So I'm giving you a choice. Beautiful, but dumb and weak. Or smart and strong, but ugly. Ugly *hair,* especially.

SANDY (frowning): Hmmm.

NICOLE: (cocking her head so that her long mane of naturally frosty curls tumbles gently around her shoulders): *How* ugly?

Unfair Sex at MIT

CASANOVA WOULD HAVE HATED IT. DON JUAN WOULD HAVE thought it was sick. Frank Harris would suspect it was somewhat exaggerated, and Aretino would have said he told you so. As for me, I thought it was historic.

What it was, was the breaking of yet another double sexual standard—this time, the old kiss-and-tell. Boys, of course, tell plenty—often more than all—in bars, fraternity houses and men's-room graffiti. Girls, it is still widely thought, do not breathe a word, let alone broadcast it. So the real question, as usual, is whether sauce for the goose tastes funny for the gander.

The specific case here involved two women students at the Massachusetts Institute of Technology (in this sex-as-science age, where else?) who recently published an irreverent "Consumer Guide to MIT Men" in a campus newspaper. In it they listed some thirty-six ex-lovers (a combined five-year total), and rated them on the basis of four stars to none ("turkey"). Everyone was identified, and no holds barred. To wit: "Four stars—close your eyes and waves crash, mountains erupt and flowers bloom"; "Two stars—don't worry about his dirty feet; they hang off the end of the bed; "One star—Lazy"; "Turkey—'I did it!' he said. 'Did what?' I ask." And the like of that.

A storm of obscene phone calls, threats of rape, and furious letters to the Institute's administration ensued—almost all of it from men *not* on the list. The president of MIT issued a formal statement in another campus newspaper deploring the girls' guide as a gross violation of "norms of taste." An administrative officer (female) experienced a feeling of nausea, although support for the authors came from other college women, both within MIT and without. A few of the listed men wrote good-humored responses, and some of the higher-rated ones had cards printed up with their "Consumer Guide" reports, and passed them out on ladies' night at a local tavern.

But a week later, stung by serious charges ranging from invasion of privacy, libel, cruelty and offending a significant portion of the community, down to and including "rot in our fine school!" (from an alumnus, class of 1911), the paper ran two apologies and an author's explanation. ("I was hoping to increase the sensitivity of men—all men, not the ones mentioned . . . by showing them how it feels to be treated as a sex object . . . All I was really trying to say was that Olympic-event-style sex is stupid, empty, and unfortunately happens a lot.") By then, however, it was too late. Local and national news media from Boston to New Zealand had picked up the story and run with it as a juicy sex scandal ("Coeds Rate 36 Males; Campus in Furor"). Disciplinary action was taken against the two women and the male editors who had approved their story—despite the fact that one only rated two stars ("overexcited").

And what had started as a spirited prank burst into a full-blown, thorny feminist issue.

*   *   *

Clearly, the brouhaha would never have moved past haha if the women had merely kissed and told, as many men do. Their fatal mistake was in writing it down. Or, as my friend Mitzi, the keen social observer, put it, in formalizing an entrenched but informal male tradition—thus forcing another hidden sexist problem out of its closet to where both sexes had to confront it.

The fascinating and, to her, central point of the story was that the farther it traveled from MIT and the people involved, the more rage it seemed to provoke. Somehow, the good-natured humor got lost, and the sexual politics got ugly, which was not the way it was on campus.

So, here in blasé New York, I decided to ask around to see if everyone agreed that (a) what the women did was not only funny but useful, and (b) the community's reaction was humorless, uptight—and politically significant.

I was in for nearly as rude a shock as the president of MIT. My friend Pamela, who normally takes a dim view of tasteless free speech, and Mitzi the social observer were among the few who saw it my way.

"Oh, sure, it's unfair," Pamela conceded, however. "And I definitely wouldn't laugh if two men published it about women. Especially if I were on the list—unless of course I got four stars."

A male friend of Pamela's pronounced the matter crass, vulgar and of no redeeming social value. He also wondered whether the women were attractive. Generally speaking, he thought, "attractive women wouldn't be that promiscuous." Pamela and I both refrained from asking whether he thought the same rule held for men.

Ginger, my novelist friend who writes fairly candid stuff about sexual mores, was horrified by the story. When I told her the MIT women were forced out of their apartment, threatened with violence and severely punished by their school, she said shortly, "They deserved it."

"Hurtful," "stupid" and "reverse-sexist" were some of the better-tempered remarks from consciousnesses I ordinarily think of as nicely raised. But every time I asked the respondent, "What if you got four stars?," the respondent would back down with a sheepish grin. "Oh, well, in that case, I'd think it was hilarious," said one man. "Me, too," said his wife.

It was beginning to look as though taste, privacy and moral outrage had less to do with it than met the eye. What we were dealing with, instead, was protection of the fragile sexual ego.

My own son, sixteen, and a friend of his (female) fell into the trap. "I even hate to read about Woody Allen's love life," my son said. "That stuff is nobody's business." His friend, Jaclyn, nodded gravely. "It reduces people to their sexuality," she said.

But they had both laughed uproariously when I showed them the MIT article, which is fast becoming a collector's item in some circles hereabouts. "What about the fact that it's funny, and not mean?" I said.

"It is mean," said Jaclyn, "because it's funny at somebody's expense." My son's turn to nod gravely.

"If you don't have anything nice to say," interjected my other son, who is fourteen, "you're not supposed to say anything."

His brother made a face. "All I know is, if they published one of these in our school paper, and I got a 'turkey' rating, I'd swallow my face."

"Aha!" I cried. "But what if you got four stars?"

He grinned sheepishly. Jaclyn grinned too. Even the fourteen-year-old, who never grins, grinned. "Well, in that case—"

"The defense rests," I said.

An hour later Jaclyn called me up to say she'd changed her mind and now agreed with me. "It's all about men's egos!" she cried. "And until recently, women weren't even allowed to *have* egos! That's why it's such a shock! But it's a good shock.

It's like the women are teaching men a lesson, the way parents have to. It's like, 'This may hurt a little, but it's for your own good. When you grow up, you'll understand.' "

"Do you still think," I asked her, "that it would be awful if they did something like this in your school?"

"Oh, no!" said Jaclyn. "I think it would be *wonderful.*"

A few days later I flew up to Cambridge to visit the beleaguered department of "consumer affairs."

"If you had it all to do over again," I asked the two women, and their male editor friends, "would you?" They looked at me with the sadder and wiser eyes of college kids who have been to war. "No," they said quietly. It had hurt when they laughed; feminism often does. I said what happened proved their laughter was important—it had shaken their world. They were no longer sure that was a good thing. But I am.

O Tempora!
O Mores!
O Prom!

'Twas the night of the prom
And all through the school
Not a feminist was stirring,
It wouldn't be cool.

APOLOGIES TO CLEMENT MOORE, BUT SENTIMENT, ORCHID CORsages, dyed-to match shoes and boy-girl role playing have all just turned up alive and well in my kids' high school, and if I weren't still suffering from a lumpy throat over pictures of Queen Elizabeth II in her golden coach, I'd really be upset.

I hear one girl wore a black dress to this prom, and one liberated daredevil showed up in pin-striped pants and a vest, but all the rest were in flowing pastels, wobbly heels and floral offerings pinned to their serene straplessnesses.

What's more, the boys rented tuxedos, called for and delivered their "dates," and shelled out upward of $100 apiece for tickets, drinks, dinner, cab fares and 5 A.M. breakfast at the Brasserie.

How could this have happened right here on East Eighty-ninth Street, where everyone I thought I knew was being raised to rebel against stereotypes, open their own doors, be assertive about their sexual needs, and go "Dutch"?

How, indeed. Cecily, aged fifteen, is in the tenth grade, where, according to my son the junior, *all* the girls take stuff like proms very seriously. Cecily was "asked," as they still say, over a month ago, and she was really excited. "It was just like the images we were all brought up on," she said. "You know, like in old novels and parents' yearbooks."

"But, Cecily," I protested, "those images were before the women's movement. When girls were being 'sweet sixteen' and 'coming out'—not to mention being made of sugar 'n spice and everything nice."

"I know," sighed Cecily impatiently, "but it's only just this once. It's like being in a little play, with costumes. Besides, it's fun. I never danced in a long dress and high heels. I never danced in anything but jeans and sneakers."

Gwendolyn, being fifteen and a half, was more blasé. "It's not really about romance," she said. "It's about staying up all night and getting bombed."

I wondered wryly whether that couldn't be done for less than $100—minus the rented tux and the dyed-to-match shoes.

"Oh, it *could,*" said Gwendolyn wisely. "But then parents wouldn't think it was sweet and adorable. This way, they do."

That was it, of course. Parents. Parents are intensely pro-prom. Mothers fuss over the accessories. Fathers fuss over whether the boy is calling for the girl, and whether he's paying for her ticket, and whether he's bringing her home in a cab. The play, with costumes, is being performed before an adult paying audience. It's a revival, always popular in times of social upheaval.

Remember how it was when we were young? Look, dear,

nothing has changed, after all. Mary Jane may be pre-med at Harvard next year, and Jennifer pre-law at Princeton, but tonight they are dressed in lavender and new lace, just as we were, and whispering about the sweaty palms of the boys they came with, and whether Trilby's strapless gown will stay up, and why Solange is spending the entire night in the bathroom, emerging only at half-hour intervals to prove that she still looks perfect.

Parents who are worried sick about Daphne being on the Pill, and Melisande swearing she wants to be "child-free," and Letitia taking up martial arts, and Hilary reading Sappho, are not only relieved, but touchingly grateful, to be wheedled out of $200 for a peach organdy formal and permission to dance all night with a well-scrubbed boy in a rented midnight-blue bowtie. The very sight of a single dewy carnation, surrounded by baby's breath and tinseled ribbon, pinned to a daughter's sweetheart neckline, may do more for a chauvinist father's peace of mind than anything short of his wife quitting her consciousness-raising group and enrolling in Total Woman.

On the other hand, why blame the parents? Maybe the kids are just part of an insidious plot, like everyone else these days. In a recent nationwide survey, 4,600 seventeen-year-olds wrote essays on woman's role in society—and half of them said they thought her place was in the home. About 7 percent explained that they thought this because "that's the way it is." Among the girls, only a scant majority—58 percent—thought women should work wherever they want. When you read statistics like that, you realize that a prom is not just a prom —it's a teen-age backlash.

My son the junior didn't go to the prom; neither did any of his five closest buddies. They all searched their souls and wallets, and decided the whole idea was a pointless anachronism, a waste of money, and offensive to their notion of "how things ought to be."

Rumor inevitably had it, among the more cynical tenth-grade girls (who couldn't go unless specifically invited by a junior or senior), that anyone who boycotted the event on either feminist or philosophical grounds was probably a phony—either a cheapskate or a geek who couldn't get a date. This view didn't quite square with the same girls' spirited defense of the prom as relaxed and unpressured—with many people going in groups or with a friend of the same sex, instead of formal "dates," and with most of the junior and senior girls paying for their own tickets. It is a well-known fact that tenth-grade girls do not have to square their views.

I asked my son what he thought the prom was all about, anyway, and he said he thought it had something to do with rites of passage. What it has nothing to do with, he added, is "real relationships." He also said that, of all the boys he knew, the ones who were most gung-ho about the prom were also the ones who could hardly talk to girls. There seemed to be a connection. There always was, of course.

In the old days the prom image was what we all had instead of relationships. We were all the girl checking her make-up in the ladies' room, and the boy with sweaty palms. Strangers on a dance floor, dressed in costumes and playing romantic leads—or trying to. The painfulness of it is still alive somewhere inside us all—along with the memories of slow music, revolving mirrored globes, pressed gardenias and cheek-to-cheek. And isn't it curious that we should be so comforted by the idea of our strong, blue-jeaned, independent, whole children clinging like waifs to the fantasy that it was all utterly wonderful?

I was heartened by the news that a few stalwart senior girls stayed away from the prom too. I like to think it was because they know you can't fight social revolutions in wobbly heels while worrying about whether your gown will stay up. I like to think that it wasn't because they couldn't get a date.

I also like to think that maybe, when Cecily and Gwendolyn

get to be seniors, they too will be thinking more about pre-med at Harvard, or pre-law at Princeton, and less about accessories. It isn't that I don't understand about tradition and romance, and the fun of dressing up, or the excitement of dancing till dawn. I do understand. You're talking to a person who not only gets lumpy-throated at the sight of a queen in a golden coach, but one who cries during old TV movies at the sight of Fred Astaire—or even Marlene Dietrich—in tails (not rented).

Well, then, am I ashamed of sentiment? Do I think all this stuff is unliberated? Am I saying that comes the revolution we'll all be wearing combat boots and trampling on orchid corsages? No, that's not it, either.

I guess what upsets me is just that, even though I believe in the Queen and Fred Astaire, I don't believe in proms; I never did. I think Gwendolyn put her finger on it when she said that a prom isn't really about romance at all. It's about acting like grownups—yesterday's grownups. When, all the while, they were acting too.

And here I'd thought that kind of play—the old costumes, roles, plot lines and all—had finally reached the end of its run.

I don't know, though. Would I feel different if I were in Cecily's dyed-to-match shoes? I hope not—but I wouldn't bet my pressed gardenia on it.

K.Y.S.L.O.O.T.O.

FEW HISTORIANS ARE AWARE THAT THE RULE ABOUT KEEPING YOUR sex life out of the office dates back to 57,628 B.C., when it was adopted as company policy in a Cro-Magnon food-gathering firm. The landmark case involved a couple of rising young zebra-bone pickers—a female called Oogh, and a male, Aagh. The two had drawn a plum assignment that included a three-day all-expenses junket away from the office, to collect an emergency winter supply of five thousand zebra bones. When Oogh and Aagh, and their highly trained staff of twenty-two specialists, failed to bring in a fraction of their quota, an investigation was launched. It was discovered that at the height of the bone-picking, Oogh and Aagh had stopped in their zebra's tracks in order to rub and tickle each other around the water cooler, or "stream," as it was then called. Inspired by their example, fourteen members of their crack bone staff had also quit picking, and gathered around to stare, point and in some cases rub and tickle each other in a crude imitation of, or "aping," as it was then called, their department heads. By the time darkness fell, everyone was either too bone-tired, as they put it, to finish the job—or too much in love to care. As a result, there was a severe zebra-bone shortage that winter, and a state of emergency was declared.

The following day a notice went up on the Cro-Magnon Company rock. It said, tersely: KEEP YOUR SEX LIFE OUT OF THE OFFICE. Or crude pictures to that effect.

Of course Oogh was subsequently fired from her job, on the ground that she had obviously distracted poor old hard-working Aagh, by walking funny. It was noted that she also wore her tiger rag in an Aagh-provoking manner. Aagh himself retained his post, on condition that he never again rub or tickle an Oogh on company time. And the vice president in charge of zebra-bone supply decided to make it easy for him by not promoting any more females to responsible positions.

(Historical footnote: The Oogh-Aagh affair did not actually set the office-romance precedent, but only followed guidelines set some years earlier in a similar incident. That case involved the now famous Adam and Eve, senior law partners in a prestigious law firm. According to the records, both parties were transferred out of the Eden office, although only Eve was stripped of her rank as senior partner. She also lost vacation and profit-sharing benefits, as well as disability pay for pregnancy under the company's major-medical plan.)

Is there a lesson here for today's executive woman? I only wish there were not. But the fact is that whatever else has changed in the corporate suite, Eros is still not an equal-opportunity employer. The no-office-sex rule still applies in 1977, and the executive female, unlike the male, still flouts it at her peril.

Over the past year a number of prominent women have afforded rich illustrations of the precise nature of that peril. Consider just a few chilling examples: 1. Isabel P——, who, as a child of eight, when asked, "What do you want to be when you grow up?," replied unhesitatingly, "President of a large and politically troubled Latin American country."

Like most women, Isabel had a hard time breaking into politics, until she hit on the idea of dancing in a Spanish cabaret which was frequented by aging Latin American strong men in exile from their politically troubled countries. With remarkable skill, Isabel managed to catch the eye of Juan P——, who saw right away that she was presidential timber. "I want you for my running mate," Juan P—— whispered hoarsely over the roar of her castanets. *"Sí, señor,"* Isabel replied with the political savvy that was later to make her name a household word across Latin America. She knew, even then, that destiny meant this to be her big chance—and Juan's Last Tango.

Juan's countrymen were horrified. "Can you feature this?" they cried. "A one-time cabaret dancer with no qualifications a heartbeat away from the presidency of a large and politically troubled Latin American country?" *"Sí,"* said Isabel, tapping her foot in perfect time to the heartbeat. *"Ole!"* said Juan. "Besides, I can vouch for her qualifications."

Ten months later Juan's old tambourine had shaken its last, and Isabel's childhood dream had come true. "I am la Presidente," she said, her eyes flashing with consummate leadership. Unfortunately, the rest of the world mistook her for a one-time cabaret dancer with no qualifications. "Oh, help," she whispered forcefully to one of her Cabinet ministers who had admired the way she rustled her scarlet taffeta skirts. *"De nada,"* he replied. In appreciation for his invaluable service to the government, Isabel taught the minister how to use her castanets. The rest of the world clicked, "Once a cabaret dancer, always . . ." and soon it was whispered that the Cabinet minister was running the country—badly. (After all, a cabaret dancer could not possibly be running the country—not even into the ground.) Isabel fired the minister and hung up her castanets, but it was too late. After eighteen months in office, Isabel herself had tangoed her last. She will be remembered, if at all, as a one-time cabaret dancer with no qualifications.

Or, as they say in politically troubled Latin America, *"La mujer no tiene el sex life en la officina."*

2. Chiang C——, who spent thirty years building up her own cultural revolution business. Like Isabel P——, Chiang C—— got her first break in the revolution game by dancing around a male comrade, Mao T——, some years her senior and already well known in the field. Through her graceful, not to say sinuous, political movements, Chiang convinced Mao that bedfellows often make strange politics. "Ah so," said Mao thoughtfully, writing it down in a small red notebook. They began to revolt so well together that Mao left his old wife, married Chiang and made her his little Red co-star. "One from Group A," sighed the Chinese people admiringly, "and one from Group B." For thirty years, Chiang figured she had it made.

But at last Mao T died—at the age of eighty-two, and Chiang moved her ceremonial teapot right into his oval office, just as the two of them had always planned. "I am Chairman," she announced. "Let's everybody get to work."

Unfortunately, the rest of the world mistook her for a one-time cabaret dancer with no qualifications. Her power base crumbled overnight like a stale fortune cookie containing the following scrutable message: "Mao say, woman who keep sex life in office someday find both fly out window. Ah so."

3. And finally, we have Elizabeth——, heroine of a juicy office-sex scandal in our very own Washington, D.C. In this case the woman, for a change, seemed to come out winners—complete with book contract, nude photo on the cover of a men's magazine, and a shiny new career in show biz, while the man in the case, Wayne H——, lost his seat in Congress.

The secret of Elizabeth's success story, however, rested on the simple, clear-cut statement she made about herself. To wit: "Who, me work in an office? I can't even type." The world chuckled delightedly. There is nothing so refreshing as a blond secretary working her way to the top (or topless)—as a one-time cabaret dancer with no qualifications.

In other words, we've come a long way since Oogh lost the zebra-bone account. A woman is welcome to keep her sex life in the office—provided she's willing to admit that her sex life *is* her office.

Uncivil Liberties

MY FRIEND PAMELA CONFESSES SHE IS NO LONGER BIG ON FREEDOM of expression. In fact, when a man in her life recently mentioned, in a dismayed tone, that some misguided judge in Ohio had thrown a man in jail for seven to twenty-five years, just for publishing a "girlie" magazine, Pamela smiled one of her most delightful smiles and said softly, "Oh, that's *wonderful.*"

I guess I have never gone quite so far as Pamela. But then, neither have I gone quite so far the other way as my friend Nancy the devout civil libertarian, who swears she would, if pushed to the typewriter, force herself to defend that publisher's right to air his disgusting magazine live and in color on prime-time TV, or on the Fifty-ninth Street Bridge during rush hour. Nancy also insists she would defend outrageous lies in advertising ("Ask Mommy to buy Old Tar cigarettes—they're good for kids!") and catchy racist slogans on the evening news, and free demonstrations of sadomasochism in front of Robert Wagner Junior High School, if not right in the science lab. In the name of our First Amendment, Nancy says, we must simply learn—and teach our children—to avert the eyes, ears and nose, much as we acquire and instruct the young in the useful habit of stepping nimbly around other public nuisances that litter the crosswalks of life in a free society.

While I was pondering that, my telephone rang, and it was a pleasant young man calling on behalf of the very magazine whose publisher had just been thrown in jail. For a brief crazy minute I wondered if he was going to offer me one of their million-dollar "modeling" fees that went begging last year after Barbara Walters, Gloria Steinem, Caroline Kennedy, Patty Hearst and other selected targets declined to answer the call. I remembered wishing at the time that they had all accepted—and then used the proceeds to buy the magazine and tear it up.

But that was not the subject of the young man's call. All he wanted was my name. Specifically, he wanted it on a petition expressing my concern at the jailing of his publisher. He assumed that no matter what I as a woman think of his product, I as a writer would force myself, like Nancy, to take up arms against his suppressors lest they light out next week after Kay Graham or Adrienne Rich—or me. In other words, all us free-press-persons should hold our averted noses and step in this public nuisance together.

By now I was feeling acutely uncomfortable. What if the fellow is right? What if they're *all* right? Pamela had to be right, because she knows that the magazine is much more than merely disgusting; it is also potent—a weapon and a textbook, not only for the very young but also for the older and more dangerous. She knows that the thing it does is teach people that women are consumer goods—Silly Putty toys with replaceable parts, or snack foods with flavors enhanced by artificial spice and color.

On the other hand, Nancy had to be right too, because she knows that the opposite of absolute freedom is, at least potentially, absolute tyranny, and because she has lived in the Soviet

Union, where there is no porn to speak of, and where all sorts of writers are routinely thrown into jail.

Finally, I had to concede, the man from the magazine was right because he knows that he's got us where we live —and what he sees fit to print has nothing at all to do with it.

Hmm, yes, well. I let my anxiety marinate overnight, and the next day I talked to my friend Charles Rembar, the attorney who escorted both Lady Chatterley and Fanny Hill to their triumphant American debuts, thereby spreading his cloak— and ours—in the mud puddle for a pack of porn hustlers. And I told him what was bothering me. I said that as a feminist I stood with Pamela all the way. But that as an American and a liberal, I stood with Nancy. And that as a writer, there seemed no place for me to stand but in the arms of a man who publishes a disgusting magazine.

"Uh-huh," said my friend the libertarian attorney. "The First Amendment junkies are out pushing again." "Junkies?" I echoed. But I already knew what he meant. If the junkies really had their way, we would all O.D. on free expression—because there would be no stopping even the classic mad false-alarmist who yells "Fire!" in a crowded theater. But the junkies can give you their solemn word that they'd put up with anyone saying or writing or advertising anything, because they know they'll never have to make good on it.

The minute our friend the publisher tried to unstaple his centerfold on TV, the network would bleep it—for fear of losing its license. And the minute he tried staging it on the Fifty-ninth Street Bridge, he'd be safely hauled away for disrupting traffic. We've got the Federal Trade Commission and the Food and Drug Administration "censoring" the man who would say cigarettes are good for kids. And public-nuisance laws keeping Lady Godiva from prancing through the midtown area, or Peeping Tom from gluing his eye to the keyholes in the Plaza Hotel. And the First Amendment junkies haven't been out waving their protest petitions to put a stop to any of it.

The truth is that we are already up to our averted eyes and ears in ifs and buts that stop us from expressing ourselves in a thousand disruptive or offensive ways. We are, after all, only *relatively* free. Which means that the rules can change as fast, or as slowly, as you can invent a newly printable four-letter word for a Supreme Court decision—or a disgusting magazine.

So there it was. Neither Nancy nor the magazine man could hold their freedom guns to my writer's head and force me to embrace that publisher—or else. When my friend the attorney saved Fanny Hill from a fate worse than publishing death, he predicted that we would have to put up with a lot of bad things. But not with *everything.*

I just wanted Pamela to know that I'm not signing the %#@!*%#! petition. And I wanted Nancy to know that my #*&#%*!#* conscience is clear.

Guilty as Charged

ESCALATING HIGH ABOVE THE PLACE ELEGANTE, CHARGE PLATE poised, shopping bags akimbo, I could easily pass for just another Regular Account. Slow payer, maybe, but Regular. No one would spot me for a hard-core Bloomingdale's freak; the kind who, twenty minutes late for her own wedding, would only be halfway down the aisle of the Young East Sider department, rummaging frantically for something new, something blue.

Oh, I got away with it. My bridegroom was still waiting, having concluded naïvely that my cab had probably just coughed to death on the East River Drive. In those days there was no way to tell him—or anyone—that you had a Bloomingdale's problem. No decent man would have married you. The truth was that I'd been into heavy impulse-buying since the age of fourteen; that I had experimented with $50 stuff marked "Not Returnable"; that by the time I was twenty I had a $37-a-week job and a $100 Bloomingdale's habit, not counting Credits and Returns. But like premarital sex and incomplete dental work, Bloomingdale's was better left unmentioned until after the honeymoon.

A few weeks ago I heard a shocking rumor about a married woman who has kept an affair going for the past year, meeting her lover only on Monday and Thursday nights so she could say she was going shopping at Bloomingdale's. The shocker for me was that she ever made it to the first assignation. I mean, think of the model rooms, furnished entirely in wall-to-wall corrugated cardboard, that she missed last summer on the fifth floor. Think of the angora sweaters she didn't find, marked down from $60 to $23 and still shedding. The free nutty cheese and sukiyaki samples she didn't get fed in the Delicacies shop. Hours of free play she could have had on 3-D tick-tack-toe sets and Japanese Pachinko machines in Adult Toys. Unlimited free use of unisex fitting rooms in the basement men's shop. Now *that's* what I call a love tryst.

I admit that mine is an extreme case, brought about, in part, by the fact that I seem constitutionally unfit to shop any place *but* Bloomingdale's. I stutter only in Saks Fifth Avenue whenever a saleslady asks me what size. It doesn't matter what size *what*. At the threshold of Bonwit Teller I begin to worry about the runs in my pantyhose. Never mind that runs cannot be seen with the naked eye through my heavy wool slacks. Never mind that I am going in only to look at handbags. On Fifth Avenue the saleswomen are trained to spot a person who has runs in her pantyhose. I am convinced they can even tell whether the runs go up or down.

At Bergdorf Goodman a registered White Russian czarina thinly disguised as a sweater clerk will ask witheringly whether she can help me. She will smile kindly, indicating we both know it is far too late for that. If one has not arrived there fully kempt, if one was not in fact born fully kempt, then surely one cannot expect *Bergdorf* to start monkeying with fate. Perhaps the sweater czarina will pay no attention to me at all, except to nod her head ever so slightly toward the gilded elevator.

The *express,* nonstop to the street level. One quite understands.

As for Henri Bendel, I am positive that the liveried doorman there is a chic ex-goalie for the Rangers whose natural reflex is to block the actual entry of persons answering my general description. (Nothing bigger than a size 6 gets in, Buzz, understand? Never mind the minks on them, Buzz, check the pelvic bones. You don't *see* no pelvic bones, they don't jut right *out* of the mink, you know right off she's a ringer.) I wouldn't say Bendel's was prejudiced. It's just that even their size 10s are a size 6.

Which brings me, exhaling freely, back to Bloomingdale's. After all, where else but Bloomingdale's could Raquel Welch have bought a billowing caftan marked "One Size Fits All," send it back because, presumably, it didn't fit all of *her,* and have it credited at once, no comment whatsoever.

Where else would Gloria Steinem submit to having her mother co-sign her charge-account application—after being called a bad credit risk (single; free-lance writer; *feminist*)? No matter that Ms. Steinem was actually supporting her mother. Liberated does not yet mean you can get along without Bloomingdale's.

Where else, for that matter, could you find—in a single week —Antony Armstrong-Jones stocking up on no-iron sheets; Marietta Tree stripping in public to try on a sequined pants suit; Mrs. Jacob Javits clutching a bulging U.S. Senate folder and confessing that Bloomingdale's takes her a whole day to "do" now (she starts at the top and works down, like a tourist covering the Louvre); two small black schoolboys pounding hard-rock hell out of a $400 electronic organ—without anyone in a suit asking "May I help you?"; nomadic tribes of fierce "singles"—all ages and sexual persuasions—sheepskin coats flung wide over silver-studded jeans, cruising the action-packed main floor for Saturday-night dates; and a pair of stringy-haired yippie-style evangelists letting it all hang out over the UP escalator rail, shouting gleefully into the crowd, "Greedy! *Greedy!* GREEDY!"

You can hardly walk through the upper floors any more without tripping over $1,000 worth of merchandise that seems to have been flung out on the floor in a petulant fit of overstock. Fat Turkish samovars and fatter Indian pillows. Old Chinese trunks filled to bursting with new fur lap robes. Thousand-dollar mounted elephant tusks and petrified ostrich eggs made into candlesticks. Ram's skulls on Lucite pedestals and lacquered blowfish permanently puffed up to $60. Everywhere you look there's another gilt-laden bodhisattva idol with a hand eloquently raised in benediction, or surrender, or possibly just beseeching somebody to stop the flow of *tchotchkies*.

You could call it an embarrassment of riches, except that it's hard to be embarrassed by anything in Bloomingdale's any more. Several weeks ago a couple of giant filthy-looking monsters suddenly appeared, glowering, near the fifth floor escalator. They were marked $2,000, the pair. "Foo Dogs," explained the label around their big ugly necks. From Thailand. Foo indeed, I thought. And dogs for sure. I would have bet my current unpaid balance that Bloomingdale's would be stuck with those sweethearts, crouching there taking up twenty-five cubic feet of prime selling space apiece, not counting the wide berth people were giving them, for the rest of the fiscal year. Some smartypants new accessories buyer has taken his last Far East junket, I thought.

Well, somebody bought the damn things. Practically the next day they were sporting matching red foo dog tags that said SOLD. The moral, if there is one, must be that if Bloomingdale's has finally gone mad, it doesn't matter, because so have we all.

Almost daily on the third floor, the Halston boutique sells at least one $450 floor-length see-through silk hanky to a lady who tosses it over her head and calls it instant elegance. Future historians may call it instant decadence, but meanwhile, whatever it is, it's selling.

And on the main floor, one of the jewelry counters has been doing a brisk turnover lately in a simple black leather belt buckled by an abstract silver teardrop, possibly as a wry comment on the price, which is $200. Luckily for at least one sharp-eyed Bloomingdale's watcher, the newspaper ad for this dubious treasure had a typographical error, so that the price read $20. After consulting hastily with her lawyer husband, the lady marched in waving the ad and demanding the belt. I hear she got it for $20, as advertised, which may or may not qualify as a ripoff.

As for the more traditional forms of *that* increasingly troublesome sport, Bloomingdale's certainly suffers its share, and probably more. Not surprising, when you consider the sprawling, informal layout, the stuff virtually rolling in the aisles, the open-rack policy in every department, including furs, and the fact that the store virtually hands out invitations in the form of those capacious shopping bags that anyone can pick up free at any wrapping counter, no purchase required. Just before Election Day in 1972, a young Republican campaigner was dispensing smart red-and-white Nixon shopping bags at the store's Lexington Avenue entrance. I personally counted a dozen passers-by who walked right past him and went inside for a Bloomingdale's bag instead.

There are uniformed store guards hovering anxiously now in the more tempting locations, and heavy white electronic "inventory control" tags have been fastened to the higher-priced soft goods, so that if you inadvertently leave the fitting room with, say, the lamé pajamas snugly tucked under your Levi's, you will definitely ring somebody's chimes.

Despite these precautions, however, Bloomingdale's salespeople say the "shortage" problem looms constantly larger. And the term "shortage" scarcely covers such minor but chronic headaches as willful damage in the furniture department, and flagrant abuse of "try-on" displays at the cosmetics counters.

It seems that every time Bloomingdale's unveils a new set

of model rooms, hordes of women having their apartments redecorated rush up to scrape the walls for color samples to take home and show the painters. How else can anyone in real life get a living room that matches Bloomingdale's?

And every Saturday afternoon, at the height of the storewide boy-meets-girl orgy, Bloomingdale's features an unadvertised "clearance" of cosmetics. Every counter displaying more than two shades of pink anything is besieged by a thundering herd of still-unclaimed girls counting heavily on free eye gloss or blushing gel to carry them through the last desperate hours before the store closes, before the last man leaves the Polo tie counter.

Somewhere on the main floor, just past the men's ribbed turtlenecks, I saw a lonely bare-chested youth, holding his purebred wolfhounds at bay, awaiting Ms. Right. She would descend, he seemed sure, any minute now from gourmet cookware, carrying a single perfect omelet pan. Together they could leave Bloomingdale's, drop off the dogs and take their rightful places on line outside Cinema I. But first she had to stop at the Biba counter and slather two iridescent layers on her lids, and two more on her cheeks, and . . .

Alas, there were two hundred other Mses. Right already lined up ten deep at Biba, at Mary Quant, at Revlon, and even at Estée Lauder's Clinique, for the hyperallergic. It sure beats going to the powder room and using your own. But by the time our heroine got to the men's shop, wolfhound boy was gone. Ah, well, there's always next Saturday.

It was, again, a scene that could only happen at Bloomingdale's. As was the one I witnessed on a quiet Tuesday morning in the Fur Den. A plump red-haired woman, obviously torn between hip-length fox and ankle-length badger, finally turned to the saleswoman for an opinion. "Where did you plan to wear it, madam?" the saleswoman began, in approved saleswoman style. "Madam" promptly broke into giggles. "To bed, probably." Needless to say, the saleswoman broke into giggles back. Just try overhearing an exchange like that at Maximilian.

I even heard a young salesman talk a male customer friend out of buying a $20 shirt. "My mother has one of these," he whispered. "I'll lend you hers."

What it all signifies, I think, is that Bloomingdale's, at the ripe age of one hundred, may be the only store in the world that doesn't act like a grownup. Which means that neither its customers, nor its remarkably bright and pleasant sales staff, feel that they have to act quite grown-up, either. It must mean something that when women in their 30's and 40's call each other up for lunch dates, they say, "Afterwards, let's go and play in Bloomingdale's." Obviously one should not examine too closely what it *really* means. Society infantilizes women? *Bloomingdale's* does? In any case, nothing about the place seems fully adult, except the prices. According to *Women's Wear Daily,* the retailing industry bible, Bloomingdale's is rumored to have the highest markups of any department store in New York. It may or may not be true, but only Bloomingdale's still delivers for free, and picks up for free, and cheerfully takes back all kinds of things that no one else would, and never tacks a "service" charge on your unpaid bill, the way other stores do. Bloomingdale's merely sends you increasingly stern "reminders" on louder-and-louder–colored paper indicating their growing displeasure with you, and finally threatens to take away your very charge plate. For many children, including me, that sounds like a much worse punishment than having Ma Bell cut off my phone.

When I was literally a child, growing up in New York, I didn't think Bloomingdale's was a real store. Going shopping in a real store was a very big deal which involved wearing your best clean underwear and being taken downtown, by your mother, in a taxi. You went to Lord & Taylor for a "good" coat, or to Saks for a party dress, or even to Best & Co. to stand on line in the Lilliputian Bazaar and talk to a Santa Claus in whom you never had the slightest confidence.

Whereas Bloomingdale's was only where the nurse had to stop and order "supplies" on the way home from your tap-dancing lesson. "Supplies" consisted of big oval cakes of soap, and Bloomingdale's Own Brand toilet paper, and striped maid's uniforms and quilted mattress pads. You never saw ladies in fur coats on the escalator. Mothers occasionally telephoned Bloomingdale's about their supplies, or their bills, but as far as I knew, the only people who went there in person were other nurses dragging other children around Housewares or Linens, and somber elderly women, in Red Cross shoes with holes cut out for their bunions, buying House Dresses.

I knew the Notions department by heart before I was ten; that was where you went to match the buttons you lost off your "good" coat from Lord & Taylor. I knew the basement, too; that was where nurses bought orange stockings and shiny peach-colored girdles for themselves. Mothers, who wore none of those articles, bought lingerie at Saks or Bonwit's. Children's underwear, however, could be picked up in Bloomingdale's as long as you were stopping there for "supplies."

I also got to know Housewares pretty well. They used to stock a dozen different brands of silver-tarnish preventive, and a dozen kinds of polishing cloths to use on the silver when the preventive didn't work. They still have most of these items, along with scores of other special brands of cleaning compounds that cost approximately twice as much as anything you see in the supermarket. I have always believed implicitly that any cleanser Bloomingdale's sells will ferret out twice as much hidden dirt. This is undoubtedly why I have never dared try any of them.

Still, I know what it says on all the labels of those magic bottles. There was nothing else to do but memorize them while I waited for the Housewares saleslady to call "upstairs" and verify the nurse's signature on my mother's charge account.

I assume that all this early training was what led me to think that "real" department stores were for Ladies—fur-clad, grown-up Ladies—and that only Bloomingdale's was for grubby little girls with skinned knees and broken sock elastics. Real stores might let me in on special occasions, if accompanied by a fur-clad parent. Bloomingdale's would let me in any old time. Even with safety pins holding up my slip. Even when—if ever—I grew up.

So as soon as I was old enough to borrow my mother's charge plate, I marched straight into Bloomingdale's Young World and bought myself two pairs of knee socks. "Charge, please," I quavered. Open Sesame. The saleslady went to call upstairs and verified my signature. Look at me, I exulted silently, I'm a customer.

It appears that a vast number of other children have also grown up, or refused to, along with the country's "Number 1 Neighborhood Store." *Somebody* spent over $100 million in there last year. According to *Women's Wear,* which reckons sales volume in relation to selling space, every square foot of Bloomingdale's did about $225 worth of business. Probably, as *Women's Wear* put it, "the best showing of any major quality department store in the land."

Inevitably, some of us have begun to wish "our" store would stop being quite such a phenomenon. Why can't they quit switching things around every week, for instance? You get dizzy just looking for the nice department where you last bought a blouse, only to find that the entire section has vanished, and they've moved all the walls to put in some funky boutique full of wax candles shaped like hot dogs and French-fried potatoes.

A friend of mine who recently returned to Bloomingdale's after a five-week trip to Europe was helplessly adrift on the second floor one day when two salesgirls sporting white carnations hove into view. "Help," she cried to them, "I'm lost." "Oh, dear," replied the salesgirls, "so are we!"

Some of us don't want it to be called "Bloomie's." Some of us would just as soon it didn't moonlight on Saturdays as the grooviest dry cocktail party in town. There is already a small but noticeable "Bloomie's backlash" of customers who haven't set foot in the place since it turned into, as one deserter put it, "Bendel's East."

"Who wants to get all spiffed up for *Bloomingdale's?*" wailed a member of my women's consciousness-raising group, who closed her account and quit cold turkey just before Thanksgiving.

On the other hand, a young bachelor I know retorts, "What *else* is there to get spiffed up for? Nobody goes to the theater any more. Or out to dinner. Nobody's even giving a party—Bloomie's is the only party left."

Another woman noted uncomfortably that "Bloomie's" newer, younger, skinnier salesgirls now look spiffier than the customers, and that if you walk into, for example, the new Yves Saint Laurent boutique looking not quite, well, "together," you're apt to get a fishy-eyed stare and the shortest shrift this side of Fifth Avenue.

"You'll never get into that, with *your* bosom," my friend Josie was told crisply one day in the bathrobe department. Josie cringed but rose gamely to the challenge and buttoned herself in. "Hmm," said the salesgirl, even more crisply. "I never thought you'd get into that, with your *bosom.*"

Undaunted, Josie bought the robe. "I'll never give up Bloomingdale's," she vowed loyally, "but let's go to the shoe department now. The thing I like about the shoe department is that they never make remarks about my BOSOM."

The store's dapper president, Marvin S. Traub, believes all of us can still squeeze in somewhere at Bloomingdale's. The bare-chested youth with the wolfhounds, sharing a men's dressing room with the girl he just found in the cheap-jeans section. And my friend Josie, and Raquel Welch and Gloria Steinem, and by all means Jacqueline Onassis, who, I'm told, wears a very *un*-put-together tan raincoat, low-heeled shoes and dark glasses when browsing in "Bloomie's" (exactly the same low-profile costume that Garbo used to affect, for browsing in Saks).

Marvin S. Traub smiles expansively, and his eyes twinkle behind the constant curl of his pipe smoke. Someday, he is confident, the bare-chested boy will button his shirt and head upstairs for no-iron sheets, like Tony Armstrong-Jones. And his girl will move up too—from cheap jeans and the Biba brigade to Place Elegante.

As for me, I have slowly come to realize that I'm not really kidding any more when people ask me why we've never considered moving out of New York to some peaceful green exurb. "What, and leave Bloomingdale's?" I cry. It used to be good for a laugh. Lately, I notice, people just nod without smiling. I'm afraid they understand.

The Switching Hour

EVER SINCE NORMAN LEAR'S TV SHOW ABOUT SEX-ROLE REVERSAL went on the air, I've been worried. *All That Glitters,* for those who never stayed up past *Mary Hartman,* was another soap-satire, in which powerful women ran the world, and men were reduced to cleaning it, going for its coffee, or just hanging around it looking cute.

What worries me is not the idea, which is brilliant, but the fact that it didn't work, and nobody quite knows why.

Actually, *All That Glitters* and I had a love-hate relationship. Which means I couldn't just turn it off and forget about it. On the contrary, I couldn't stop watching it or talking about it. I kept wishing I could kick the TV to fix the actors, or the dialogue. It embarrassed me that I cared. As a consciousness-raiser, I wanted it to outbunker Archie. Yet every night while the set *Glittered,* I wished it would go out and come back when it grew up.

Sex-role switching, for better or worse, is certainly catching on. In fact, if the trend continues, we may need a vaccine for it by 1984. Not that it's new, exactly. Like most revolutionary ideas, it's been around for centuries. We all know that men played women's roles in Shakespeare's day. The Bard's own plays were full of make-believe sex reversals, and the comical, tragical or farcical results therefrom. Virginia Woolf toyed with the theme in *Orlando*. I played with it myself in my last novel, *A Sea-Change*. Even my psychiatrist husband has been using sex-role reversal as a technique for therapy. He says it's a quick, if not painless, way to learn how the other half lives, in a troubled relationship.

In 1977 an apprehensive male novelist, Robert Merle, perpetrated a painful "what-if" fantasy, set in a near-future state of totalitarian feminism. As in Thomas Berger's *Regiment of Women*, oppressed or endangered males are mistreated by fanatic "women's libbers." It's probably highly significant that when Merle's book was first published in France, it bore the ironic title *Protected Men*. But for the United States the name had to be changed—to protect them more? We're not ready, it seems, for "protected men" here—not even ironically. So the American edition sported a straight *macho* title: *The Virility Factor*.

Meanwhile, off-Broadway, in Eve Merriam's delightfully sly musical conceit, *The Club*, seven women in top hats and tails strut lightly as turn-of-the-century male chauvinists. They tell harmless (?) sexist jokes and sing authentically silly ditties about ladies fair and not so. But the satiric point was sharp enough to make some male critics wince, and to bewilder a sizable share of its mesmerized audiences. Controversial or no, *The Club* became a solid hit, and Norman Lear promptly invited Eve Merriam to be a consultant for *All That Glitters*.

She was there when they developed the characters of the mad househusband, the tough boss-lady, the philandering wife, the lecherous appliance repairwoman and the female Arab tycoon, complete with harem boy. But even Ms. Merriam thinks the actors could have used a marathon "body workshop," in which they'd have learned to get more in touch with the opposite sex within themselves. (The female cast of *The Club* worked endlessly on masculine body language, until the gestures, frowns, sneers, lip curls and raised eyebrows became second nature—so convincing that audiences actually forgot they were watching women.)

But *Glitters* was not doing impersonations. The women looked and dressed like women—glamorous hairdos, pretty clothes, make-up. The men—well, the men looked and dressed more like gay men: skin-tight slacks, open-necked shirts, body jewelry, elaborate blown-dry hair styles. Only the househusband, Bert (played by Chuck McCann), dressed like a slob—gender irrelevant. As the counterpart of the middle-aged wife who's let herself and her marriage go to pot, he was utterly believable. At an early screening, which I attended along with a dozen teen-agers from the High School of Performing Arts, the consensus was that if *Glitters* were all about Bert the househusband, the show would be a smash.

Unfortunately, *Glitters* was a woman's world—with the emphasis on Bert's wife, Christina (Lois Nettleton), and the other tough, hard-driving executives of Globatron Corp., a giant industrial conglomerate. And as tough, hard-driving executives go, they could all have taken lessons from the late Rosalind Russell, or even the late Joan Crawford as Mildred Pierce, not to mention Everett Sloane, Sydney Greenstreet or H. R. Haldeman. In *Glitters,* Barbara Baxley, as L.W., alias Big Shot, mustered up a pretty good snarl and a passable cobra smile. And Marilyn Sokol, as the Arab tycoon, was silkily, inscrutably perfect. But the rest of the ladies were just that—ladies. Bitchy, perhaps, but nowhere near "man" enough for the job.

I can't swear that a dose of testosterone all around was all the show really needed. The teen-agers I watched with thought there were more problems than that. "Nothing *to* it except the gimmick," said one. "Women holding chairs out for their male dates. Women staring at the legs of scantily dressed waiters, or grabbing their guys' pectorals. Male secretaries being chased around the boss's desk. That's all there *is*. There's no *story.*"

"But if the gimmick worked," I said, "wouldn't it be enough?"

One girl, age seventeen, sighed. "Maybe," she said, "for my kid brother. He's thirteen—and he could stand to have his consciousness raised, the little b——."

Around the country, *Glitters* fared unevenly, I hear. In the Midwest and Far West, where it was shown in the early evening, the ratings were high. Young kids are watching, and they thought it was hilarious. In the East, where it was aired at 11:30 P.M., hardly anybody got hooked enough to wait up.

Feminists, for the most part, were either confused about the show or disappointed. Some expected it to be an idealistic view of a future world in which everybody was liberated from everything. But after seeing an episode or two, they worried that the show would give liberation an even worse name than it already has, in some quarters.

"I can just hear the men now," said my friend Pauline the activist. " 'If that's how women in power behave, just like the worst men, then why in hell should we give it to them?' "

On the other hand, as my friend Janice the optimist says, "Isn't there something great about a TV show in which two middle-aged women are talking on the phone, and they're not gossiping about diets, or face lifts, or men who got away? They're plotting about where to deliver the five million dollars, and how to save the hundred-and-twenty-five-million-dollar ad campaign! Isn't there something absolutely *wonderful* about tuning into that?"

Yes, so help us, there was.

Court One

Don't play tennis with women—even lace-pantied ones. It's bad for the ego . . .

—BENJAMIN FELSON, M.D.
Medical Opinion & Review,
November 1965

AFTER UNDUE CONSIDERATION, I HAVE DECIDED NOT TO TAKE UP tennis this year. Although it is the nineteenth year in a row that I have made this same decision, I don't mean to imply that I ever make it lightly. On the contrary, I make it downright heavily, especially now that tennis has become a warm-weather feminist issue.

It was probably a feminist issue back when Gussie Moran flashed her lace panties on the court (see above), and it almost certainly was when women tennis pros demanded equal pay for equal play. And God knows it was when TV caught Billie Jean King whipping the unlaced pants off Bobby Riggs, as frenzied chauvinist millions cheered.

But out where I live in the summer, tennis only recently became a feminist issue when the club at which the tennis-person in my life plays adopted a rule forbidding women to play on Court One. Ever. If all the courts in all the world were empty, and it was January, and it was midnight, and a hurricane had eaten the net, and all the male players were in jail for income-tax evasion, women would not be allowed to play on Court One.

Now, at this particular club, women also may not play on any of the eight *other* courts during what the male players decree is Prime Time (Friday afternoons; Saturday, Sunday and holiday mornings, and Saturday, Sunday and holiday late afternoons). At this particular club, women are the Not Ready for Prime Time Players.

For the record, I have personally examined Court One. It is a nice court; nothing special. It is the kind of court which, if you didn't know that women weren't allowed to play on it, would never capture your imagination, let alone mine.

But last year, in the heat of my annual decision-making process about whether or not to take up tennis, I found myself gripped by shameful fantasies involving Court One. First, there was the fantasy in which I myself was playing on it, alone against the club's entire board of directors, I had my racquet between my teeth, and a litter of Siamese kittens tied to each ankle, à la Bobby Riggs, and I was lobbing my opponents to death before they dragged me off.

Next, I fantasized Billie Jean herself coming out as my weekend guest, and the tennis-person in my life trying to arrange a friendly foursome for an exhibition match. In this fantasy, he and Billie Jean show up at the club, only to find forty-six male bondholding members lined up, racquets aimed and loaded. All of them are wearing T-shirts whose little embroidered alligators are eating women tennis champions.

Finally, there was the fantasy about a player who, in actual real-life fact, got to play on Court One three years ago, as a full-fledged member. Fellow named Dr. Richard Raskind, it was. But in the fantasy he comes back as Renée Richards, waving her latest chromosome test at the board of directors. For once they are aced on their own Hartru turf, and Court One is declared permanently unplayable on account of bad publicity.

Chances are, none of these wonderful things will happen this summer. The women who play at this club—wives, daughters, companions and guests of members—will go on playing by the rules, or not at all. One wife, I hear, is now a strong enough player to beat most of the men. Some of them will even play with her—in non-prime-time, anywhere but on Court One. And she will remember to thank them.

As for the men themselves, they will go on stoutly defending the rules as altogether proper for a club where "serious weekend tennis" is seriously played by busy and important people. Though nowhere in the constitution is there a telltale phrase like "men only" or "men's club," the gentleperson's agreement is that it's just that. So long as there's a rule about Court One, any woman who can beat a man at his own game will have to do it discreetly—on a back court, where fewer of his peers can witness it.

And the men will continue to explain (to each other) why this is important. Tom says he doesn't feel free to "let go and be himself" (say naughty words? throw his racquet? throw a tantrum? lose?) when there's a woman on the court. Dick explains that the "quality of the game" is affected: he can't or won't hit the ball as hard at a woman opponent. And Harry, who's on the board of directors, insists that no woman could ever qualify for full membership because she'd never get past the "tennis committee" that judges members' playing ability. And if she beat every man on the tennis committee? "Why, then she'd be blackballed by the membership." So it goes.

Or, as the husband of the club's strongest woman player

recently quipped, "Right now, there's only one woman who'd want to be a full member—and I've got her safely locked in the attic."

I once asked one of the regular women players—not the best one—how she feels about playing at this club.

"I'm . . . comfortable," she said uncomfortably.

"You are?" I asked.

"Well," she conceded, "not when the hostility shows. Like the time my ball accidentally rolled on their court, and one of them kicked it away—viciously. My partner just bit her lip and ran after it, but I felt really angry."

" 'Comfortable,' " I echoed softly.

She smiled. "Hmm. I suppose if I'm not part of the solution, I'm part of the problem, right?"

I smiled back.

Now that I've made this year's decision not to take up tennis, I realize why I feel so free to get exercised about Court One. Unlike the women who play in such clubs, I have nothing to lose. I can fume all I want about the unfairness of it all, but it's they who are vulnerable. They—and the male tennis players in their lives.

Sometimes I pick on the one in mine. I say to him, "You're a feminist, why don't you do something?" And he struggles with the answer. "Because you don't play," he says. "And I can't go fight a war for other women who haven't asked me to—and who aren't fighting it for themselves. If one of them were ready to take a stand, I'd stand with her all the way."

"Even if they unstrung your Wilson T2000?" I asked him.

"Even if they took away my topspin forehand," he said. "But the ball's not in my court." And he is right, of course.

Before I was born, my mother went to a fortuneteller who told her I would grow up to be a tennis champion like Alice Marble, the first woman player of whom it was said, admiringly, "She plays like a man." (In those days, that was still a compliment.) At times like this, I wish the fortuneteller had called the shot better. I like to think that if she had, I'd be out there right now, liberating Court One.

Hey, you think maybe next year I ought to take up tennis?

Under the Influence

NOT SINCE THE WHITE HOUSE FIRST TOOK TO LISTING ITS ENEMIES have so many names come up, or been put down, for other people's eyes only. Top threes; big fives; all-time, all-time fifties—lists are now the fast food for thought recommended for those who must restrict their ordinary intake of hard news.

Besides, there's something so crisp and tangy about a nice fresh list of ten. Ten anything—à propos of nothing.

Which would explain why, the minute I heard that a Washington newspaper was calling up random authority figures to name America's Ten Most Influential Women, I couldn't wait to play.

I understand that almost everyone they called mentioned Rosalynn Carter and Betty Ford, more or less in that order, but then they seemed to get stuck, or else to start quibbling defensively—either about the meaning of "influential" or about the definition of "woman." (One respondent, a man, confessed he was so hard pressed to think of ten real, live, influential, American women that he wound up including Mary Hartman, Edith Bunker and Rhoda.)

It seemed to me the trouble started as soon as they said Rosalynn Carter, who, though *potentially* influential as all get-out, had not yet caused the slightest ripple in the national lifestream.

However, when I mentioned this to my friend Dilys the sophisticate, she said I didn't understand. "An influential woman," she explained patiently, "is one who makes a dent in the pillow next to the leader of the Western world."

"Oh," I replied, my crest rapidly falling. "I sort of hoped that *wasn't* what the poll takers had in mind." (I wonder if a Russian would consider Mrs. Brezhnev an influential woman. And did we ever think Pat Nixon was? How about Nancy Kissinger?)

Over the next several days I worked feverishly on my own private list, consulting with Significant Others of various persuasions. The results were, as they say, mixed. My teen-aged sons offered me Dear Abby, the lovelorn adviser, and Jeane Dixon, the astral interpreter. A male culture elitist paused, sighed and finally murmured, "Twyla Tharp?"

Two sage eleven-year-old girls zeroed in on Farrah Fawcett-Majors, which I thought made staggering, if nonfeminist, sense. After all, FF-M has single-headedly set the new standard for American male erotic fantasies—and for American female attempts to act them out.

Other fairly predictable entries included television's own Barbara Walters, Total Woman's own Marabel Morgan, liberated woman's Friedan and Steinem, and *anti*-liberated woman's own Phyllis Schlafly.

Among a certain jaded midtown group, the name Jacqueline K. Onassis kept popping up, with apologies, because of her persistent influence on something called "style." A few younger Beautiful People pushers countered with Diane Von Furstenberg, the wrap-tie-print princess. As one supporter put it: "Her dresses may be ugly, but she *makes* style—she doesn't just *have* it."

There was intense disagreement about whether Barbra Streisand qualified. Some said she was merely "a Hollywood product." Others declared heatedly that she (1) "gets her own way" and (2) "didn't have a nose job."

Powerful women agents, literary and theatrical, had some heavy support—notably Lynn Nesbit on the East Coast, and Sue Mengers on the West. No writers, though. And no other "stars."

As for influentials in the sexual arena, they ranged from Helen Gurley Brown, inventor of the "Cosmo girl," to Virginia Johnson, discoverer of the multiorgasmic woman. There were some Johnson detractors—on the ground that she wouldn't have influenced much without her co-discoverer, Dr. Masters. On the other hand, the same thing was probably said in France about Marie Curie.

A few solid Mother's Day votes were cast for Lillian Carter, for being so refreshingly unlike any of our previous matriarchs, including Rose Kennedy. My friend Violet, the controversial playwright, said Miz Lillian is already the Farrah Fawcett-Majors of her age group—because she's the first presidential mama who ever refused to keep her opinions to herself, or her seat glued to a White House guestroom rocker.

I suppose it was discouraging that nobody came up with a sure-fire political influential who wasn't firmly attached to a male leader. Scattered returns for Representative Barbara Jordan, Governor Ella Grasso, Lieutenant Governor Mary Anne Krupsak and mayoral ex-candidate Bella Abzug. But the ironic question was, If "influence" really does mean who gets to whisper in a President's ear, then how come the names Midge Costanza, Patricia Harris, Mary King or Juanita Kreps failed to roll trippingly off anybody's tongue?

Anyway, I've finished *my* list, and am prepared to defend it. Ten Most Influential American Women:

1. Billie Jean King, because she proved it was okay to play with the boys—and win.

2. Ellie Smeal, the new president of N.O.W., because she calls herself a "housewife," which may revolutionize the women's movement—this time for keeps.

3. Mary Tyler Moore, because she was TV's first grown-up woman, and she got away with it.

4. Margaret Mead, because she's been there all along.

5. Kay Graham, the newspaper publisher, because she can match grace under pressure with the best of them.

6. Lily Tomlin, because as my poet friend Mary says, she's the first funny girl who ever forced us to take her seriously.

7. Mary Wells, the advertising executive, because she doesn't think like a man—she just thinks big.

8. Joni Evans, the publishing executive, for the same reason.

9. Katharine Hepburn, because.

And 10. Rosalynn Carter . . . because?

Sanjay's Complaint: A Psychohistory Lesson

- "When a woman becomes devilish, she beats all the records. Now, I can't say that she [Mrs. Gandhi] is all devil . . . but the good is suppressed and the devil is on top."—INDIA'S NEW PRIME MINISTER, MORAJI DESAI
- "Indira was the only man in the cabinet. She'll be the only man in the Congress now."—MRS. VIJAYALAKSHMI PANDIT, INDIRA GANDHI'S AUNT
- "I'm sorry, Mom."—SANJAY GANDHI

THREE EMINENT PSYCHOHISTORIANS HAVE ALREADY FINISHED INTERpreting the results of India's election, in which Indira Gandhi and her son, Sanjay, fell from grace and out of political power. Dr. J. S. Mindblow of Harvard, whose book went for $1.2 million, concludes that Indira lost because she was possessed by an orthodox Hindu she-devil. Dr. R. V. Doppelgang of Yale, whose total package of hard- and soft-cover rights went for $2.1 million, diagnoses Indira as an ordinary victim of raging or aging female hormones, which gave her son an acute gender-role identity crisis.

And Dr. Tatiana Moxie, the only woman in the group, whose book will be produced on TV as a major mini-series to air opposite *Laverne & Shirley,* claims that all "psychohistory" is false, including this one. According to Dr. Moxie, the cause of Indira's downfall was that she was a bad mommy.

All three doctors were interviewed last week at the offices of their literary agent, who also represents Isabel Perón's personal maid and two poodles, said to be in exile somewhere in Argentina.

Mindblow has amassed impressive evidence proving that Indira Gandhi is the reincarnation of the goddess Shakti (Divine Mother) in the terrible form of Bhavani, who doesn't stay home with her son but goes out to become a guardian deity for thugs, thereby creating national cataclysms and disasters on a large scale.

Doppelgang's research, however, leads to the inescapable conclusion that any woman of a certain age who wears a soft sari and carries a big state of emergency will cause arrogance, ruthlessness and zealous misbehavior in her son. This in turn will create national cataclysms and disasters on a large scale.

But perhaps the most startling thesis is Dr. Moxie's notion that the mother-son relationship lies at the root of all Third World political trouble. In the Gandhis' case, Moxie discloses, Sanjay was a "Spock" baby who was permitted to chew betel nuts, which were bad for his teeth. Indira also apparently forced the boy into intensely competitive Little League yoga, before he was old enough to meditate on the eternal verities. As a result, Moxie contends, Sanjay grew up constitutionally unable to chew betel nuts while assuming the lotus position, which in turn led to national cataclysms and disasters on a large scale.

All three books fairly bristle with fascinating Indian lore about curried rice, buffalo demons, erotic temple carvings, the obligatory peek inside Indira Gandhi's medicine cabinet, and explicit material about betel nuts, designed for frank discussion on the *Merv Griffin Show.*

In a poignant incident, for example, Moxie relates how, after the election returns showed Indira losing by an overwhelming margin, Sanjay offered to write "I have been arrogant, ruthless and zealous" 500 times. Indira, cloistered and surrounded by sycophants, sent word that she would accept it only if he wrote "I have been *very* arrogant, ruthless and zealous." Sanjay, to no one's surprise, stayed in his room chewing betel nuts and reading *Oh! Calcutta!*

Mindblow's controversial "demonic possession" theory seems, of course, the most crassly commercial of these books. Mindblow himself notes, in a touching foreword, that this marks the first time believers in such phenomena as *Rosemary's Baby* and *The Devil in Miss Jones* will have a serious work of political theory to call their own. He hopes it will spark a new literary genre, and proposes that it be called, simply, *Possession Politics.*

As for Doppelgang's book, women will no doubt recoil from its "raging, aging hormone" thesis as blatantly sexist nonsense. However, he does offer us the first persuasive explanation of Sanjay Gandhi's strange enthusiasm for forcing 700,000 of his countrymen to have vasectomies. Doppelgang observes that Sanjay must have known the forced sterilization program would *hurt his mother* (italics his) more than any of her other notorious "disciplines." Predictably, Doppelgang blames the program on Sanjay's unresolved Oedipal complex. "What else could it be?" asks Doppelgang rhetorically. Most readers will be hard put to think of an answer.

Of course no definitive psychohistory of the Gandhi story will be complete without an extreme feminist view, which has yet to be written. We can, therefore, look forward to at least three more books, propounding the following theories:

1. As a child, Indira's political genius was tragically thwarted by lingering male prejudice against girl tyrants.

2. Sanjay resented being the only arrogant, ruthless, zealous boy in his class who had a working mother.

3. The powerful betel-nut industry, which is 98 percent male, tends to blame older women and working mothers for national cataclysms and disasters on a large scale.

Mother Loving

THIS IS A CAUTIONARY TALE ABOUT MOTHER LOVING. THE KIND that dares not speak its name; the last taboo; the ultimate dirty word.

When I first met them, four years ago, Pat and Mike were a perfectly ordinary mother and son. Close, but well within the bounds. Mike's father was long gone. Mike had never known him, and Pat scarcely remembered him. She had had a fair number of lovers before and since, and several other children, all grown. Only Mike was still with her. And then one day, all of a sudden, Pat and Mike became more than just mother and son.

Unthinkable. Inconceivable. How could they? I don't know —how does any taboo get shattered? Someone shatters it, that's all. Anyway, they did. Mike became his mother's lover. And the world didn't end. In fact, impossible as it sounds, I swear to you they never seemed at all troubled by what they were doing. They were shamelessly affectionate in front of people. They also quarreled openly. Yet I never felt uncomfortable when I was with them. Their relationship seemed, well, natural. It made a transcendent kind of sense. One almost felt guilty for one's lingering shock. Fathers and daughters, yes. We've all read about those. But she was his *mother*!

Mike had never loved anyone else in his life. In that respect, you could argue that Pat had taken a terrible advantage of him. He never had a chance to find a "normal" partner his own age. It was clear that this had never occurred to Pat. Unbelievable selfishness. Unthinkable. Inconceivable. A mother exploiting her son for her own sexual gratification. All right, it was monstrous. The gods would have to exact punishment. The world would have to end.

I wish it hadn't. But the truth is, Mike was just not much of a lover, by Pat's standards. She considered him, not to put too fine a point on it, lousy. At first she had been tender and patient, as any mature woman would be with a young, inexperienced boy. But practice failed to make perfect, and finally Pat couldn't stand for Mike to touch her. They were . . . sexually incompatible. The harder Mike tried, the more anxious he got about it, and the more cruelly Pat rejected him. It was awful to watch them together. She was his *mother*!

Pat took on a lover who bore a striking resemblance to Mike, even to the red hair. Ironic, perhaps, or possibly just mean. She never tried to hide what she was doing. Mike saw them together. So did a lot of people. He never reproached her. It seemed to their friends, including me, that he didn't really understand what she was doing. He just assumed that she still loved him, and that everything would work out. After all, she was his mother.

Whenever Pat went out to meet a lover, Mike would sit around the house waiting for her to come back. And when she stayed home, he sat around waiting for her to be nice to him. She wouldn't let him come near her. If she spoke to him at all, it was only to snarl some torrent of abuse or contempt. He stubbornly refused to get the message. They reminded me of a movie in which the girl really loves the guy but knows she's no good for him, and that's why she's got to make him go, for his own sake. But the fool won't give her up until she convinces him that she hates him, that she never loved him at all. Maybe I'm giving Pat the benefit of too many doubts. But I couldn't believe she was simply rotten. After all, she was his mother.

What finally happened was that Mike went crazy. Couldn't eat, sleep or anything. All his bodily functions stopped functioning at once. His doctor said there was nothing physically wrong, and he was put in the hospital for observation.

After a few weeks Mike appeared to be completely recovered. The doctor sent him home. The instant he walked through the front door, Pat snarled something at him, and he lost control of his bladder. The doctor said it was clear that Pat was Mike's problem, and that he must leave her, or be destroyed.

That was about a year and a half ago. I haven't seen Mike since, though I hear he is living with an elderly woman on the Upper West Side, and is all right.

Pat had three lovers after Mike left, but never stayed with any of them for more than one night. Last spring she had a hysterectomy, and since then has had very little interest in sex. She seems content otherwise.

The wages of sin is probably not death, but a miserable sex life. Or maybe it's just that a pair of short-haired domestic cats are not the ones to shatter the incest taboo. In any case, as I interpret the tale of Pat and Mike, this seems to be the caution: You can have love or a mother. You cannot have both.

Porn for Women; Women for Porn

THE HAND-LETTERED CARDBOARD SIGN, POSTED OUTSIDE A NEW peep-show parlor in Manhattan's fashionable East Fifties, bore the usual enticing message: ADULTS ONLY. Underneath, in smaller, cruder letters, the management had scrawled what it considered a liberated afterthought: *Women Also Welcome.*

Now, why in the name of male bonding would a smart young smut peddler with a choice midtown location want to let *women* in? Imagine it: Women riffling through his pile of $10 imported bondage magazines as if they were so many striped percales at a January white sale. Women snooping around his notions counter, giggling at the plastic "love aids" and pointing rudely at the life-size inflatable dolls with the rubber balloon-filled orifices. Women hogging the 30 Movieolas 30, elbowing the male regulars out of the way and popping their hot perfumed quarters into the slots for a quick peek at "Torture Chamber" and "Young Girl Does It with Very Old Guy." Women asking for their money back if not completely satisfied. Women Also *Welcome?*

Sexism aside, it was clearly a sign of the times. The pornography industry, solemn protector and leering nurturer of man's most secret and profane sex life, is suddenly trying—with all the fumbling urgency of an adolescent lover—to go coed.

It was probably inevitable. Once blue movies such as *Deep Throat* and *I Am Curious (Yellow)* became a shockingly respectable, if not boringly chic, diversion for sophisticated mixed audiences; once frontal male nudity flashed successfully on and off Broadway; once Marlon Brando talked dirty and performed simulated sex acts in a major box-office $5 reserved-seat hit, it looked as if we were finally willing to go all the way. The men who know pornography best felt it was high time the ladies learned to appreciate the art of the folded raincoat.

Though no one has yet dubbed them "boyie" magazines, the seventies have brought us at least three slick fun-and-gamy publications designed to do for women what *Playboy* and *Penthouse* presumably do for men. *Viva, Playgirl* and *Foxylady* all feature male nude pinups—centerfolded, coyly posed and genitally exposed—plus a dizzying assortment of titillating articles and advice on sex-related topics: pubic hair styles and crotch-watching *(Viva);* how to use a bidet *(Foxylady);* and why orgasmic women should be kinder to premature ejaculators *(Playgirl).*

Besides the magazines, there are books that reveal women's secret erotic fantasies, and X-rated movies whose ads, aimed at a mixed audience, attempt to soothe nagging female guilt feelings about enjoying voyeurism with the menfolk. Two instances: "Lets you feel good—without feeling bad" *(Emanuelle),* and "The first erotic film about love" *(Wet Rainbow).*

So far, however, women's response is not so hot. *Viva* magazine lost $3 million in its first twelve issues, though its publisher, Bob Guccione, who also publishes *Penthouse* for men, declared that *Viva* had been "marginally in the black" for months.

Some women who read these magazines protest that they do so *despite* the male nude pinups, which they find either silly or irritating—not sexy. Are they lying? Or merely repressed? Are they secretly turned on but not admitting it to themselves? Are younger women more stimulated than older ones?

The answer is some or all of the above. Women do lie about their sexual response; they always have. Only the content of the lie changes from one generation to the next—from the Victorian woman denying *all* response to the loving wife faking orgasm to please her man. What a woman *says* she feels—indeed, what she may very well *think* she feels—still depends to a dismaying extent on what the dominant (male) culture expects of her at the moment.

Psychiatrist Mary Jane Sherfey has described this phenomenon as a persistent problem in research about female sexual response: "One wonders if this well-known difficulty women have in reporting their sexual sensations does not stem from the fact that they deceive themselves and us about the nature of these feelings because they are afraid that what they *do* feel is not what they *should* feel."

At present, what women may think they "should" feel is sexually liberated. They "should," we are told, take their multiple orgasm where they find it, and let the meaningful relationships fall where they may. They "should" also turn on to crotch-watching and vibrators for quick release from sexual tension. They "should" rise above their fear of flying, hang up their hangups about needing love and a half-hour of foreplay, and, finally, buy matching his-and-hers pornography for the bathroom magazine rack.

If it all sounds like the plot of some well-thumbed male erotic fantasy, it is no wonder. Drs. Phyllis and Eberhard Kronhausen, the wife-and-husband psychoanalysts who study pornography laws, were on to this plot back in 1959. "In keeping with the [male] wish-fulfilling nature of obscene writings, the female characters . . . are just what men would like women to be: highly passionate, sensuous and sexually insatiable creatures who like nothing better than almost continuous intercourse."

Classic porn always described men in a satyriasis-like condition of permanent sexual excitement, the Kronhausens observed. And the women in classic porn stories were perpetually "on the prowl for a new sexual partner, or a new sexual experience."

But if the "new porn" for women is really men's sexual fantasies warmed over—if it offers, in fact, no truer picture of women's erotic desires than *The Confessions of Lady Beatrice* —then why is the stuff selling at all?

Rumor has it that much of the women's sex-magazine readership is actually made up of male homosexuals because they, at least, find the male nudes sexy. When a character in *The Ritz,* a Broadway comedy set in a gay steam bath, exclaimed, "I can't *wait* to see this month's *Viva!,"* the line got a big, knowledgeable laugh.

Many women, especially young, liberation-hungry women, buy one or two issues out of curiosity, or go to a porno movie whose twenty-two-year-old female star gives interviews saying she got into the business because porno movies excited *her* sexually. Thousands of women will read another woman's book whose heroine pursues erotic equal rights by what used to be called sleeping around. But when the novelty of such "new" notions about female sexuality wears off, women in general don't get "turned on."

Why not?

I talked to a number of women about the pictures in *Viva* and *Playgirl.* These were typical reactions: "Maybe I'd like them better if the men looked more *masculine . . .* " "Maybe if the penises were *erect . . .* " "Maybe if the poses were more *erotic . . .* " Maybe. Women who have seen male homosexual pinup magazines describe those photographs as somehow more sensual and appealing than the ones in *Viva* or *Playgirl,* if only because it is evident that the photographer, model and magazine editors all think of the male body as an erotic object —and know how to present it as such.

Still another complaint by women who are turned off, rather than on, by the *Viva-Playgirl* male nudies, is that where a naked couple appear in an erotic "photo-essay," the two never seem remotely like lovers. The pictures often have a soft-focus romantic-dream quality, but as one woman put it, "There's no sexual tension." Nakedness is not enough.

Neither, it seems, is naked sex in action (as in the peep-show parlors, which show what one male film critic calls "industrial documentaries"—piston-and-pump genitals doing their thing) or the new crop of X-rated "sexploitation" movies aimed at middle-class mixed audiences. Though curiosity—or a nagging husband—may propel a woman to go once or twice to a *Deep Throat* or *Behind the Green Door,* the experience rarely makes a hard-core fan of her.

Molly Haskell, a film critic and author of *From Reverence to Rape,* a study of the treatment of women in the movies, believes that what is missing for women in the typical porno flick is the same ingredient left out of the women's sex magazines: believable sexual tension between a man and a woman. There is no seduction, virtually no romantic suspense, and only perfunctory "foreplay" (kissing, caressing, sensual interaction). Women moviegoers, says Haskell, are "profoundly aroused by observing the total man-woman relationship"; they are much *less* stimulated by watching narrow-focus genital contact, which is, of course, the essential core—whether hard, soft or medium—of the blue movie.

Some women felt cheated after seeing *Last Tango in Paris* because Brando never took off his clothes. But many others responded strongly to the eroticism portrayed in the film because they were *already* turned on to Brando. In fact, some women have said they would have been less aroused by the sight of a nude Brando whose body failed to match the Adonis in their Brando fantasies.

To many sex researchers, women's lack of response to the "new porn" comes as no surprise. After all, American women have, technically, always been "also welcome" to buy, read, collect and be erotically stimulated by pornographic material. Books, pictures and films depicting male genitals and nude sexual acts have been more or less freely available to any woman willing to ask for them—under the counter, through the mail in plain brown wrapper, at seedy stag-movie houses, or in the private collections of male aficionados willing to share. Yet few women ever bothered to ask for such material, and until recently, few men thought they ever would. It had been widely believed, by pornographers, by experts on sexual behavior, and by both men and women in general, that women were somehow biologically immune to porn; that their lack of pleasurable response to "dirty" books and pictures was a permanent condition of their peculiar sexual character.

In 1953 the *Kinsey Report on Sexual Behavior in the Human Female* presented impressive statistical data supporting the view that a woman could not be sexually aroused by seeing pictures of nude bodies, or even by seeing a man's penis in the flesh. Any man who attempted to excite his female partner by showing her his etchings was, the Kinsey researchers warned, bound to be disappointed. But lest he take her lack of response personally, the report noted that it was "characteristic of women in general" to be unmoved. In fact, a glimpse of male sex organs might actually inhibit a woman's sexual response.

There were, however, some glaring inconsistencies in the Kinsey portrait of woman as a psychologically unmovable sex object. For one thing, the women studied were *strongly* aroused by movies—not X-rated stag films, but ordinary "commercial" romantic movies. Indeed, they were erotically stimulated more often, and often more intensely, than men were. The Kinsey investigators recognized this as a reaction to the romantic action portrayed, to the portrayal of some particular character or actor in the story; to the "emotional atmosphere" of the movie as a whole, and in some cases, to the woman's feelings about the man with whom she was watching it. This concept of "romance," rather than graphic portrayals of genital sex, as "women's pornography," has been noted by a number of other prominent researchers. Dr. Robert J. Stoller, the author of *Sex and Gender,* defined pornography as a daydream which induces genital excitement in the observer, chiefly through three essential ingredients: voyeurism, hidden sadism, and masochism. Stoller noted that "women's pornography," which includes true-romance and confession magazines, and probably advice-to-the-lovelorn columns, may deal with seduction, rape, adultery and all sorts of illicit sex, but the *manner* in which such acts are presented is, as Stoller put it, "so subtle as to be completely overlooked by the men who write pornography laws."

Women and young girls in various studies have reported intense genital response, even orgasmic response, to such diverse psychological stimuli as popular song lyrics, television soap operas about illegitimate pregnancy, and most of all, to the rich visual imagery of their own erotic daydreams—sexy pictures to be sure, but privately screened, and often starring everything *but* the genitals.

In the post-Kinsey generation of sex research, numerous small-scale experiments—mostly by men—have focused on every imaginable aspect of women's and men's responses to pornography. Among them:

• Whether guilt and anxiety affect women reading erotic stories. (*Finding:* They did feel guilty, but they also felt aroused.)
• Whether husbands and wives respond similarly to erotica. (*Finding:* Yes, and the more "authoritarian" the marriage, the more *both* spouses were sexually aroused by, and also more

sternly disapproving of, pornography. "Egalitarian" couples were both less aroused and less disapproving.)

• What kinds of erotic films produce the highest degree of female arousal. (*Finding:* Films showing male-female romantic sex rated highest, followed by mildly erotic group sex, explicit sadomasochism, and male homosexuality. The women tested preferred, and were significantly more stimulated by, films in which a man related to a woman, even if cruelly.)

• Whether a woman's sexual fantasies and desires increase during the twenty-four-hour period after seeing porno films and slides. (*Finding:* Yes, about as much as men's did.)

• Whether any mechanical device can be devised to measure a woman's immediate genital response to visual erotic stimuli, the way male response is tested by before-and-after measurements of penile circumference and acid phosphate levels. (*Finding:* A vaginal tamponlike probe, equipped with a light and a photo cell, can now measure increased blood volume in the vagina, revealing whether the woman experiences sexual arousal while viewing a sexually explicit film.)

All this elaborate attention has yielded a bewildering mass of often conflicting data about how a woman's sexual arousal takes place, but no clear answers as to why, even with newly permissive social attitudes toward her sexual activity, she still doesn't appreciate good old-fashioned, genitally focused, man-made porn.

Kinsey didn't take into account the crucial role played by repressive cultural influences in shaping sexual response; the Kinsey report on women took it for granted that whatever was discovered about how women reacted to psychological stimuli was biologically determined. Since Kinsey, however, a number of theorists—again, mostly male—have swung to the opposite extreme, tending to blame inhibiting cultural forces for everything women feel—or don't feel—that differs from men's feelings.

This theory rests on the assumption that the usual male response to the sexual parts of a woman is the norm, though in fact it is as much a "conditioned" reflex as a woman's. A boy is taught that women's breasts, thighs and buttocks are instantly exciting, just as a woman is taught that men's penises are not to be looked at or thought about.

Yet the cultural-conditioning theory is most often applied only to women. If women were sexually freer, it is suggested, we would turn on as automatically to the sight of—or even the word for—a man's crotch, or its contents, as men do to ours.

In other words, the assumption here is that women need to be culturally retrained, and that men are the ones to do it. Porn thus becomes a kind of visual teaching aid, representing sex as the all-American genital contact sport, complete with rules and code signals.

The coach knows enough not to expect his rookie players to warm up the first time out. So the game plan is to give them time—and more training. After all, the theory goes, if you keep telling a woman it's now okay to look, and you keep pushing those pictures at her, and you let her know you *expect* her to turn on—then, by God, she'll make it. She will, in effect, meet the male standard of sexual response. "Instant-on," just like a television set. Unless, of course, she has a problem.

It is certainly true that despite the lightning speed with which women have quit worrying about frigidity and taken up worrying about multiple orgasm, their conditioned negative feelings about genitally focused sex cannot possibly vanish in a one-night stand at the skin flicks.

But the fact is, cultural repression is *not* the whole story, any more than biology was. There is, for instance, substantial evidence concerning the key role of the male sex hormones (androgens) in the sexuality of both men and women, and of gender-related differences in the erotic arousal process itself. Much of this information comes from the work of Dr. John Money of Johns Hopkins University in Baltimore, author of

Man and Civilization, and co-author with Dr. Anke Ehrhardt of the State University of New York of *Man and Woman; Boy and Girl.*

Money and Ehrhardt accept the premise that both men and women can be equally stirred by, say, a nude picture, but they explain that what goes on in the woman's erotic imagination differs fundamentally from what occurs in the man's. This is their description of the difference:

The man sees the girl in the picture as an object of desire. In his imagination, "he takes her out of the picture and has a sexual relationship. He may masturbate. It is not unheard of that he may make a genital aperture in the picture and put his penis through it, and then masturbate."

A woman seeing the same picture may be just as intensely stimulated by it, but in a very different way. Instead of taking the image out of the picture, Money says, she "projects herself into the image," and identifies with the female body on erotic display. Her arousal is then directed toward a particular man toward whom she feels "romantic affection." (Money doesn't theorize on what happens if the woman viewer is a lesbian or bisexual. I interviewed several bisexual women on this question, and all reported that they see the woman in the picture first as a sexual object, and only secondarily as an image with which to identify. One bisexual woman I talked to added that when she sees a picture of a man and a woman making love, she identifies with the man, and imagines herself arousing the woman.)

But what if the picture shows a sexy man? According to Money, most heterosexual men will not be stimulated by it, and neither will most women—because they cannot identify with or project themselves into the image of the male figure. Thus nobody will find the male nude erotic, except a homosexual male who is attracted to it as a sexual object.

Some psychiatrists, however, take strong issue with Money on this point. Dr. Robert E. Gould of New York City, who works with mixed-couples and men's groups on changing sex roles and sexual consciousness-raising, believes that as men become liberated from *their* conditioned sex roles—and *their* hangup about genitally focused quickie sex—they will be able to see their own bodies, and the bodies of other men, as both erotic and esthetically appealing. As of now, Dr. Gould says, most men are still "too threatened by the specter of homosexuality."

Could that be why the male nudes in *Viva* and *Playgirl* seem so unsexy? Very likely, Dr. Gould says. "The male editors and photographers don't—or *can't*—let themselves turn on to the erotic potential of the male bodies they're displaying." In a recent interview Bob Guccione, the publisher of *Viva* and *Penthouse,* described the charged, seductive atmosphere that he tries to achieve before shooting pictures of a nude female for *Penthouse.* He claims to spend three days building up the model to a pitch of sexual tension where "you literally have to hold her at bay." It is hard to imagine Guccione talking that way about how to get the sexiest picture of a naked man.

Dr. Gould also noted that the male models selected for *Viva* and *Playgirl* often have unusually large penises. This concern with showing men as "well-endowed" is typical of classic male pornography—and represents the notion held by men in general that a large penis equals sexual prowess and potency. Women have no such illusion—and no such interest in oversized penises.

This might explain why, though thousands of women saw *Deep Throat,* few remember the name, face or any other distinguishing feature of Harry Reems, the actor who played opposite Linda Lovelace. Unlike the male star of an ordinary romantic movie, Reems failed to give women viewers a character to fall in love with. His penis may have given a tour de force performance—but *he* did not.

The more one examines such evidence, the more one sees that the issue of woman's "failure" to respond to porn has less to do with woman than with the men who are trying so feverishly to excite her. There is nothing wrong with the female arousal mechanism, but something is clearly wrong with a male pornographer who can't seem to produce a decently sexy picture "for women" to save his box office or magazine. It almost begins to seem as if they don't really *want* to.

In the course of researching this article I interviewed fifty women, including erotic artists, psychiatrists and sex researchers, housewives, college women and a number of writers whose fiction or nonfiction work, like my own, has often focused on women's erotic feelings and responses. This test "sample" was as large as many, and larger than some, of the research experiments that make up most of the "medical literature" on women and pornography. Most of my interviewees were in their thirties; a few in their twenties, forties or fifties.

Nearly all of the women in my sample agreed that depersonalized, "genitalized" sex, as represented in all classic male-oriented pornography, does not, and probably never will, appeal to women. Most of us did not know a single woman who had been "reached" by the "new porn for women," for the simple reason that, as one woman put it, "it's nothing but porn for men—in drag."

Before speculating on the future—if any—of a genuine women's pornography, I asked each interviewee to name one movie scene, photograph, work of art or literary passage that she personally had found intensely erotic.

The only "classic" pornographic work cited as a "top turn-on" was *Story of O,* by Pauline Réage (generally believed to be a *nom de plume* for a male author). A deeply masochistic literary fable involving a woman's degradation and willing submission to sexual enslavement, *Story of O,* a best seller in the 1950s, was one of the few pornographic novels ever to "reach" an enormous female audience.

Several women reported being most intensely aroused by paintings or nude sculpture, notably Goya's "Naked Maja"—

a nude woman clearly offering her body erotically to an unseen man; Rodin's nude lovers embracing, and Donatello's bronze David—a slender, almost androgynous youth, standing with one foot delicately poised on the giant severed head of Goliath. (The women who found this statue highly erotic explained that it seemed to represent their ideal of male grace—an exquisite, fragile balance between power and an almost childlike vulnerability.)

One woman said her favorite adolescent fantasy centered on certain Byron poems and letters; she imagined Lord Byron himself making oral love to her while writing them. Another recalled a poignant Genet film that showed two male prisoners reaching hungrily toward each other by kissing and sucking on a straw forced through a chink in the wall between them.

A young novelist described the seminude photograph of a body-building champion in the book *Pumping Iron*. It showed him posed in a darkened theater flexing his muscles, smiling to himself, and wearing only brief trunks and a white fedora tilted rakishly to catch the light. The appeal of this picture, explained the woman who found it so powerfully erotic, lay "not in the perfect Mr. Universe body, but in the secret grin under the brim of the hat."

To most of the women, a movie scene was the most vividly recalled "turn-on." Most frequently mentioned, in descending order: Clark Gable carrying a struggling Vivien Leigh up the stairs in *Gone With the Wind;* James Mason looming menacingly over Ann Todd in *The Seventh Veil;* the wordless rape scene in *The Fountainhead;* lesbian sequences in certain pornographic movies such as *Defiance* and *Flesh Gordon;* Gregory Peck lasciviously observing Jennifer Jones's rear end as she scrubs a floor in *Duel in the Sun;* Marlon Brando's silent rape of Maria Schneider in *Last Tango in Paris;* Barbra Streisand reverently—and longingly—touching a sleeping Robert Redford in *The Way We Were*.

A strongly recurrent theme in these reports was romantic

masochism—the cold, cruel or indifferent man, and the woman who endures it because she "can't help" loving him. Psychiatrists have said this is rooted, like most "rape fantasies," in a woman's guilt or anxiety feelings about wanting sex. Feminists have added—and some psychiatrists agree—that women will get over these fantasies once they acquire a positive, assertive self-image. But masochism continues to be a strong component of most women's erotic imagery; sex therapists in my sample confirmed that this is invariably true of their patients.

Next to romantic masochism, the most frequent element in all the erotic highlights mentioned was a mood of tender sensuality, often conveyed through lingering body caresses—whether between a man and woman, two women, or even two men. The strong attraction to lesbian love sequences was often reported by women whose personal "real life" orientation was totally heterosexual. The psychiatric view of this phenomenon might be that the woman who responds so intensely to a lesbian love scene probably has strong, though latent, homosexual feelings. Another view—one advanced by the women themselves—is that what they are responding to is the overpowering tenderness of such scenes, which, unlike many passionate heterosexual love scenes, almost never contain violent or hostile undertones.

In describing and explaining their own erotic responses to movies and art, these women may well have provided all the essential clues about the future of "porn for women."

It may bear a striking resemblance to the kind of total-body sensual focus currently being taught to sexually troubled couples in sex-therapy clinics, such as those pioneered by Dr. William Masters and Virginia Johnson. This "sensate focus" approach—rather than the old male pattern of zeroing in on the genitals—is what women's erotic response is all about.

If the sex therapists succeed in teaching men that caressing, massaging and nongenital touching can afford intense erotic gratification for both sexes, then perhaps there is hope that men—including pornographers—will eventually stop thinking of these movements as mere time-wasting "foreplay" leading up to the main coital bout. Once men are "turned on" to the idea of sex as a bigger picture than a close-up of genitals on the peep-show Movieola, we may all get a totally new kind of "human porn"—or better still, no porn at all, because we'll be acting out our own best fantasies.

Combat in the "Adult" Zone

WE SEEM TO BE IN A CHURCH. IT IS DARK AND SILENT. SOLITARY huddled figures—lost, seemingly in prayer—stand transfixed before small religious articles and books, or lined up with bowed heads along two rear walls, their faces pressed against mysterious black boxes that emit flickering light but no sound.

In the center stands a large elevated wood platform heaped with bills and coins in neat piles; behind it a man, priestlike, is dispensing change. He is pale and solemn, expressionless, as befits his station.

The gloom lightens and we see that it is an "Adults Only" store—indeed a kind of church for the hard-core believer. Everyone inside is male. Only the religious articles pertain to the female: inflatable dolls, books, photos, films, "love aids."

Suddenly the voices of live women pierce the silence. A flicker of fear and loathing passes over the stone face of the manager on the platform. The male patrons whirl around in panic, folded raincoats clutched to their bodies like shields. Two women hover at the doorway.

MARGE: Millicent, look at the sign: "ADULTS ONLY—*Women Also Welcome*"!

MILLICENT: Oh, Marge, I've never been in an "adult" store! You wanna try it? After all, the *mayor* tried it.

MARGE: Well . . . you think it's *safe*?

MILLICENT: It's got to be safer in there than out here on the street. I mean, in there at least you *know* the person next to you is a maniac.

MARGE: Yes, but will they think we are too?

MILLICENT (looks at her friend doubtfully): I sure hope so. Better hunch over or something.

MARGE: Female maniacs don't hunch over.

MILLICENT: How do *you* know?

MARGE: I'm guessing.

MILL: Well, then I'm hunching.

(They edge inside the door, blinking.)

MARGE (loudly, to anyone): Uh, sir? The sign outside says *Women Also Welcome*?

MANAGER (to himself): Women. Don't that beat all? Tryna run a nice clean operation here, alluva sudden the boss decides we ain't "liberated." *Women* are "into" sex now, he says. You ask me, they oughta be a law against it. Equal rights? My wife ever set foot in a place like this, I'd take my #2 leather strap, the black one with the little knots, and I'd—(Catching himself) Uh, yes, ma'am?

MILL: Er, is there a place to check our coats?

(Four men whirl around again, terrified, holding on to their raincoats for dear life. Mingled cries: Check our *coats*? They wouldn't *dare*. Nobody checks Rico's coat, unnerstand? Nobody. The manager restores order; raincoat men scurry back to their posts, clutching and hunching.)

MARGE (browsing at the notions counter): Look at these little, er, gadgets, Millicent. I hear Clovis got one after her divorce.

MILL: How does she like it?

MARGE (shrugs): Oh, you know Clovis. She's crazy about it

—but she's afraid to make a lasting commitment.

(As they talk, more and more men move away from them —recoiling—so that soon there is a great clearing of empty space around them, as if they were Martians in a bleak alien landscape. For the most part, they remain oblivious to this ostracism.)

MANAGER: Ladies, uh, perhaps you'd like to step back here and visit our, uh, foreign-film section?

MARGE (cautious): What's playing?

MANAGER (patient): Everything, lady. This week we got your basic torture and degradation; your flouting of deep-seated cultural and religious taboos; your schoolboy crushes on rubber, leather, fur and double-knit polyester; your cute but badly trained animals; your depraved baby girls preying on unsuspecting middle-management executives . . .

MILL (dreamily): Got any handsome young men with, ah, mature ladies?

MARGE (dreamily): Maybe a lady sultan with a male harem?

MILL (really timid): Or a nice *kissing* scene with just Robert Redford?

MANAGER (suspicious): Lissen, what kinda place you think this is, lady?

MILL (anxious): Oh, let's just try the one with the cute animals, Marge.

MANAGER (relieved): Right this way, ma'am. This is a fine new Scandinavian film, one of our best. You got your, uh, heroine romping and cavorting with her horsie, her doggie, her frisky lambikins and her fluffy little chickie.

MARGE: Her *chickie*? Ycch!

(The manager hustles them quickly past "occupied" machines.)

MARGE (reading): That one sounds good—*Swedish Massage* —Rub-a-dub-dub!

MILL: Oh, I hate it when they're dubbed. I'd rather see it in Swedish, with subtitles.

MANAGER: Here you are, ladies. *"Paws*—see Kong's girl tame wild horsie, doggie, lambikins . . ." (They fumble with change, murmuring): My treat! Oh, no, *you* paid for lunch, Marge; No, I *insist*. (Finally the quarter gets deposited.)

MARGE: Can you see, Mill? Maybe we should take turns. (Man at next machine groans.)

MILL: Sssh, Marge, watch the picture. Look, here comes the chicken part.

MARGE: Oh, dear. (Half covers her eyes, like a child peeking at a scary movie.)

MILL: I don't think I understand her motivation.

MARGE: I wonder if the ASPCA reviews these.

MILL: Actually I think it's kind of cute. Look how it's eating right out of her hand.

MARGE: Oh, Mill, that's disgusting. Imagine what Cleveland Amory would say.

(Suddenly the picture clicks off; the screen goes dark.)

MILL: Is that *all*? Where was the frisky lambikins? I didn't see any frisky lambikins.

MARGE: Maybe the horsie played two parts?

MILL: No, I'm positive. There was *no lambikins* in the entire picture. Look— (They read the sign posted on their box.) ". . . horsie, doggie, lambikins . . ." See? Marge—this is a clear case of consumer fraud.

MARGE: Listen, Mill, I don't think they give refunds in here —even if not completely satisfied. (Millicent is already marching toward the manager's platform.)

MILL: Is that true? No refunds?

MANAGER (nervously): No refunds.

MILL: Even if not completely satisfied?

MANAGER (shouting): Satisfied? Nobody comes in here to get *satisfied!* What kinda place do you think this is, lady?

MARGE (pulling Millicent toward door): Come on, Mill, I know when I'm not wanted.

MILL (crisply): Well, I'm reporting this to the Department of Consumer Affairs.

MANAGER: Consumer Affairs? What is that, a French picture? (As they leave, male customers close ranks. Manager follows women to door, reaches outside for his ADULTS ONLY sign, and slowly tears off the bottom half, which contains the line *Women Also Welcome.* At this, there is an audible sigh of relief from the men. A few wave their rumpled raincoats in triumph. Outside, we hear the women's voices.)

MARGE: Hey, Mill, what d'ya say we get out of the "adult use" zone and go to a sexy movie?

MILL: Hmm, did you ever see the one that opens with Ginger Rogers lying in a huge white satin bed, with satin sheets, a satin nightgown . . .

MARGE: I know, and she's lying there tossing and turning, and there's this crazy seductive tapping sound on the ceiling right over her—*ssh, ssh*—it's a soft-shoe . . .

MILL: Yeah, it's Fred Astaire! And then you see him, he's taking off his white tie . . .

MARGE: And he smiles that funny crooked smile, and—

MILL (moans): Oh, Marge, don't say any more. I'm . . . Oh. Ooh. Ahh.

City Mouse, Country House

SHE BROILS NOT; NEITHER DOES SHE SWIM. IN THE HAMPTONS, THIS alone may constitute a violation of local ordinances. What is such a person doing in a waterfront house, surrounded by tennis fanatics? She allegedly sits indoors, willfully pale and lacking in muscle tone, not to mention fully clothed, when all about her are out perspiring freely, inhaling fresh chlorine, and getting evenly burned on the backs of their knees.

Does she at least *try* to play tennis? Let me put it kindly: she still has trouble following the bouncing ball in a sing-along.

Perhaps she putters around the garden, enabling her husband to mumble, "Oh, she's home mulching," and thereby gain a few sympathetic nods. But people out here do not regard a promising avocado pit in the kitchen as a sincere effort. If push comes to shove, she cannot even read outside in an adjustable lounge chair, because the sun makes her eyes water, and the umbrella is all the way over there, and if she gets up, the lounge chair will snap irrevocably into the fetal position.

Then what *does* she do out here all summer? "Nothing," however true, is not an acceptable answer. The fact is, she cowers behind a flimsy typewriter turning out damp pages of wintry urban prose that seem to wilt in the humidity and salt spray, like her hair.

In the Hamptons, it is widely assumed that if you are a woman with a family, and not out playing any of the other summer games (or reading in the sun), then you must be contentedly playing summer house, which is the only approved alternate activity, like arts and crafts for the summer camper who got dizzy on the Bear Mountain trip and threw up her entire hiker's lunch just below the peak. In camp, she could always opt for braiding guimpe key fobs when everyone else was portaging around the rapids. In camp, they made allowances.

Unfortunately, she can't seem to play summer house, either. After six years of owning one, she has compiled a partial list of the rudiments that she will probably never get the hang of. Here it is.

1. *Getting there.* It's not so much the traffic as the organizing. Every spring weekend she remembers they have run out of oregano, but she never remembers where. By July 1 they have nine jars of oregano in the country. (In the city, they have six jars of parsley flakes.)

2. *Wild life.* No, not the parties. The ants in the Granola jar. Also those in the sugar, the rice, and the three unopened boxes of cheese crackers for which there was no more room in the refrigerator on account of all the food that had to be brought out from the city lest it rot over the three-day weekend, only it is rotting anyway because first one must eat all $27 worth of fresh local produce one couldn't resist picking off the highway farm stands. (So what if the tomatoes were really shipped from New Jersey a week ago; look at the endearing way they spell ASPARGOUS.)

Wild life also includes rats that winter over in the Ivory soap (they eschew Zest, for some reason); baby field mice that the cat brings home for approval and then stashes behind the electric baseboard heater, and finally, sea gulls that picnic on top of the garage and toss their empty clamshells down onto the driveway at five-thirty in the morning.

3. *Entertaining.* Because it isn't. The first weekend of every summer, when she sees people in the supermarket gaily piling their carts with institutional-size cans of rum-punch mixers and pretzel nuggets, she says they will have to throw a party soon because it's been three years now and they will never be invited anywhere ever again. By Labor Day it becomes appallingly clear that they have squeaked through yet another summer without entertaining anything but the thought, or rather threat, of entertaining. She broods about this constantly, huddled there behind her typewriter. Brooding about it is probably every bit as exhausting as doing it. The only difference is that for brooding, she doesn't have to get up from the typewriter to clean the house.

4. *Cleaning the house.* It is said that country dirt is superior to city dirt, being cleaner by nature. It is said that, therefore, country houses are easier to keep. There is no truth whatever to this rumor, which I believe was started by a male-chauvinist group renter in Amagansett.

The fact is that country dirt is worse than city dirt, because there are all these people in the house actively engaged in manufacturing or importing dirt on a more or less full-time basis. You shall know them by their trail of tennis socks, sandy bathing suits, soggy towels and abandoned glasses full of melting ice. Why are there tennis balls in the refrigerator? (It keeps them bouncy.) Who left the fish in the garage? (Mommy did.) What is that funny smell in the living room? (The cat just brought home another dead field mouse.)

And this is not counting the dishes. In the city a writer who is also a woman with a family need not concern herself with the mechanics of more than one meal a day. Breakfast, after all, is minimal. Children take and dispose of their lunches in school. Husbands eat lunch out, and the writer herself makes do with a chunk of Jarlsberg Swiss and a Dr Pepper. Dinner is all, and even that is confined to a small, well-defined space known as the dining area.

But in the country everyone goes on a six-meal-a-day portable snacker's diet. Breakfast lasts an hour. Leafy salads are required for lunch. Frantic chopping of fresh scallions and radishes. Endless filling of frosty pitchers for unslakable thirsts. "Eating out" means carrying fifteen trays to and from the patio. Even the cat, who gets pregnant every Fourth of July, is suddenly eating for seven. Sloppily.

And why is it the children never seem to bring home a friend who eats the crusts?

5. *Shopping.* Isn't it easier to load groceries in the car than to trudge through city streets dragging a heavy cart and/or hefting an armload of bursting brown bags? Well, it looks easier, but it takes twice as long, and you can't send the kids back to get what you forgot. A bike basket will only hold so much. (I have a feeling we're out of oregano.)

6. *Children.* The single overriding advantage of having a vacation house so they can be with you all summer instead of away at camp is that you get out of sewing name tapes on 476 garments, of which only 41 will come back. On the other hand, children in a summer house are apt to hang over the typewriter asking embarrassing questions such as "What page are you on?" and "How come you never play tennis with us or go swimming?" One can always snap "Mommy's working," but by now they've worked out a response to that. "Oh," they say blandly. "Well then, can we have something to eat?"

7. *Husband.* The single overriding advantage of having a vaca-

tion house so that he can be with you instead of working in the city is that he'll play tennis or go swimming with the children, and occasionally say "Mommy's working," which somehow sounds more convincing coming from him. On the other hand, he too is apt to hang over the typewriter asking embarrassing questions such as "Why don't you come outside in the sun and read in a lounge chair?" or "What page are you on?"

As a child summering in rented beach cottages, she used to try harder. In fact, she was usually the first kid on the block to plunge into the poison ivy. She was also the one who found the yellowjacket nest, who picked the flowers that caused premature hay fever, who tripped over the croquet wicket on Memorial Day and broke her arm. She was a game little girl. She spent the best part of every summer tucked in bed with a nice set of colored pencils, moving only to scratch an occasional hive. Nobody ever asked her why she was so pale. Those were the days.

There are, of course, other ways to spend a summer. Traveling, for instance. Traveling involves remembering what you packed in which suitcase (oregano?), and being strapped into an adjustable airplane seat that doesn't even include a fetal position. Then there's sending the kids to camp, which involves not only the name tapes but also remembering what you packed into which trunk so you can keep track of what doesn't come back (parsley flakes?).

And of course there's visiting other people's summer houses, which involves explaining why it is that you don't swim or play tennis, or lie in the sun in a nice lounge chair.

Also, visiting other people's summer houses involves leaving one's own. In other words, coming out from behind the typewriter.

By the way, what page did you say she was on?

Confessions of a Health-Club Nut

AT FIRST IT WAS PURELY PHYSICAL. I SUPPOSE SOME WOMEN would be ashamed to admit that. Not me. I always believed it couldn't be bad if it felt so good, even when my mother said that was how you got into trouble. But whoever thought it would go so far? That I'd be sneaking out every day at the crack of noon, and not coming home till dinnertime; that I'd be shutting off my phone, my friends, my typewriter; that I'd stoop to making up shabby alibis when my children, my husband, my agent ask where I've *been* all day, and who with, and *doing what?*

Doing what? Falling in love, of course. Rolling around half naked on the floor of a mirrored room; performing unnatural acts in unspeakable positions; committing indecent exposure under glaring lights, not to mention the bold stares of hot-eyed strangers. Oh, I know you'll think me a fool. Who else but a fool could fall in love with a health club?

But I'm not the only one, believe me. I could tell you, for instance, about a girl with a body so perfect that she had to join a club just to flaunt the butterfly tattoo on her left buttock. I could also mention a certain plump older woman who sits and sings outside the steam room. Just sits there, in broad ultraviolet light, with nothing on but her goggles and terrycloth hairdo protector, belting out a dozen choruses of "Can't Help Lovin' That Man of Mine." Where else but a health club could she book an act like that?

Maybe you'd like to hear about the blue-haired lady in the French fishnet tights? Takes six calisthenics classes a day—*six*—breaking only once every forty-five minutes for a quickie measurement of her upper thighs.

Maybe you already heard about the well-known socialite who drops her jeans in the gym and stands on her photogenic head before dashing off to some swell midtown party where nobody knows what makes her skin glow like that.

I could tell you chilling stories about a baby-faced schoolteacher who turns into a savage beast in karate class, joyously kicking, punching and choking any strange man in white pajamas who bows gravely to her and says, "Kick [or punch, or choke] me!"

I've seen a Wall Street banker strip off his narrow tie and buckle his tiny pectorals into weird Nautilus Time Machines, in the vain hope he will come out with mind-blowing pecs like Big Arnold. Never mind who Big Arnold is. His pinup photos are all over my organic-food store, and I'd bet you a week's supply of ginseng root that *he* belongs to a health club too.

There are suspicious characters who drop by after work for a five-minute run on the Jog-o-Matic and then stand around panting for half an hour outside the women's belly-dancing class. And then there are the women who drop by to *take* the belly-dancing class. And the paranoids of both sexes who think the sauna is a hotbed of political agents assigned to find out how much everybody weighs and measures.

Have they freaked out on fitness? Hardly. At the New York Health Club, most of us merely dabble in fitness as a wholesome relief from workaday tension. I myself have never been seriously fit a day in my life, though I certainly got fed up with Atkins, and watered down with Stillman, and shaped up by Marjorie Craig, and taped down by Ann Benné. One season I turned a few isometricks, though not for pay, of course. I tried running in place and rubbing in other places: Relax-a-Cizor before it was banned, and Metrecal before it was panned. When I got into health clubbing I was still on the rebound from two incredible years with a Bullworker-Tensolator. You never heard of a Bullworker-Tensolator? Well, I can assure you the German men's Olympic squad wouldn't move a muscle without it.

I probably shouldn't be telling you all this. Some people just can't empathize with it. If I were to tell you that one day I was doing my Jumping Jacks nude in front of a mirror, and certain parts of me were still jumping ten minutes after I stopped, would you have any idea of the mental *anguish* I felt? I doubt it. If only more people knew what we went through, the world would be a little less hostile to fitness lovers. So that's why I wanted to come out of the locker room, so to speak. Maybe, when you know what went on between me and my health club, you'll understand.

YOGA:
If Your Head is on the Floor, Get Your Chin on the Floor

Unreliable sources have it that The New School may soon offer a course in yoga-and-masturbation, which will teach you how to make love in the shape of a pretzel to your own deeply relaxed knee joints. I, for one, find this notion positively redundant. Besides, if Swami Sachadanandi had meant for us to sex up the spinal twist, he would have given us an easier way to get there from here.

Nevertheless, they may well be on to something. After nine months of practicing to get my feet tucked firmly behind my ears, I am fully prepared to lie here and swear that yoga was the most exciting thing to happen to my body since the summer I got into a pair of size 7 jeans, only to find out that they were mismarked.

To think that I, a jump-rope dropout in the third grade—a person who was benched during hopscotch games, who ice-skated on her ankles, who schussed into the only tree on the beginner's ski slope—that *I* could go up into a shoulder stand —chest slammed smack up against the thyroid, taking in *prana*! Never mind that it took me from Thanksgiving to Easter before I could hold my head up while performing an elaborate backbend called The Wheel. The day it finally happened I truly felt the earth move beneath me. And as my friend Bunny, who by then could raise one leg as *well* as her head, put it, in a transcendental whisper, "It's so beautiful up here, I never want to come down!"

But in yoga, as in all of love, nothing lasts forever, and nothing is ever enough. It took me seven months to get my head on the floor, straining forward between my outstretched, quivering legs, every muscle in my body silently crying uncle. Yet the instant I felt my feverish brow graze the carpet, I heard the instructor's silken voice in my ear: "Your head is on the floor? Now get your chin on the floor!"

Clearly, yoga is the perfect S-M exercise. "No gain without pain," the teacher tells you, smiling her other-worldly smile, which you know must come from perfect discipline, shining thoughts and pure food. So I tried not to let it bother me the day I saw her in the club snack bar eating a prune Danish.

Then one day she failed to show up for class, and the entire corps de yoga, in full leotard, had to stage a protest march in the club's front office. The male substitute teacher they tried to foist on us was incapable of the most elementary half-lotus. He offered us a breathing class instead. *"Breathing?"* we shouted. "Who needs to *breathe?"*

But the most crushing disappointment came the day I got scolded for standing on my head during final relaxation. After five months of grueling, relentless practice—fighting fear, gravity and a feeling of acute silliness—I had *made it* onto my head. And now my teacher didn't care. She was no longer interested in my body. I had interfered, she said, with the vibrations in the room. She was trying to move onward, she said, "Out of the body—into *astral projection!"*

"Astral projection?" I murmured, blinking back tears.

"Just leave the shell of your body lying there on the floor," she commanded. "Send your mind to the upper left-hand corner of the room, and look down at your body."

"Never!" I cried. "I *know* how my body looks from up there. That's exactly why I'm staying down here. I don't mind chanting an 'Om' or two, but nobody's getting me out of my shell."

My yoga teacher didn't say another word, but her lips curled and I could tell she no longer respected me.

I wonder if it would have ended differently with someone who didn't eat prune Danish.

THE MACHINES:
Or, Just Show Me the Leg Curl, Please

Fifteen minutes on these babies will give you the equivalent of an hour of calisthenics. Easy.

Nautilus Time Machines! The very name conjures up echoes of submarine torture chambers; of sea nymphs in blue Danskin tights strapping their victims down on hip and back machines.

Now, then. *Pull!* Your legs are poised gracelessly overhead, held up by a padded bar. You resemble a beached sea turtle, but in reality you are a human pulley, which is more like it. You always *said* you wanted to be a pulley. The bar is ingeniously connected—by means of nautilus-shaped wheels—to a pile of ten-pound weights behind your head. You get to lift the weights by pushing your thighs against the bar. If you can do it twenty times, and your hair hasn't meshed with the gears, you get to come out.

For one terrifying instant you lie there giggling. This is not really a health club at all. It's an elaborate set for some low-budget skin flick about a mad gynecologist.

But then you leave your legs forward and they ... descend! You feel your lower back snapping smartly, the backs of your hips straining immodestly against the black leather couch. Look, Ma! your inner voice exults, No hands—and hardly any permanent spine damage!

Shucks, it is nothing but a giant Rube Goldberg gadget from outer space. There are six of them in the total system—the Thigh Machine, the Leg Curl, the Pullover . . . (Feminist note: the men's system has two more than the women's—one for the torso, one for the "delts.") Each piece of equipment is carefully engineered to train its fantastic and revolutionary powers on a specified "anatomy area." The instructors have measured you all over, in order to reach a decision about how many weights you can pull. You get to haul more and more weights each week, until your oblique measures a lean, hard 30 inches instead of a slack 32½. The only trouble is that nobody seems to know exactly where your oblique is. Did you have it when you came? Never mind, it must be around here someplace. We'll approximate. And besides, when you filled out your progress card, you did not choose to mention it under "Primary interest." Your goal, you indicated, was to be five foot nine.

Unsolicited testimonial: I used the Nautilus equipment daily for five weeks. I did not skip any of the machines, even though I hated the Pulldown (good for chest and arms) and I still can't clap the padded bars together in the Shoulder Row (I did it once and couldn't stand the noise). My leg bicep is now 16 instead of 16¼. My oblique seems to have moved unaccountably upward to where the last instructor measured for "underarm," but I don't think that's the fault of the machines.

Oh, and I'm still only five foot seven.

DIET:
Or, Seduction, Betrayal and Forbidden Fruit

"For friendly diet advice," said the diffident little notice posted in the club snack bar, "a qualified dietitian is available."

The thing is, there was never any *one* dietitian available. Everybody in the club, including the locker-room attendant, went around dispensing friendly diet advice at the drop of a pound. Behind the receptionist's desk I found the resident expert on vitamin B-6, kelp and lecithin. "Lecithin is more," she said firmly. Since she looked to be about a size 9, there was no doubt she was qualified.

I wasn't so sure about the masseuse, though. "Eat what you like, don't worry nothing," seemed a trifle glib, coming from a size 14½ mesomorph, Albanian or no.

I was assured, about three times a week, that Billie Jean King weighs 135 pounds, and is only five foot three and a half, because muscle weighs more than fat. Yet nobody ever seemed to know what Billie Jean King eats.

The yoga crowd—those who taught it and those who were merely "into" it—were more or less strict vegetarians. Animal flesh (they refer to it as "carcass" so it'll sound more disgusting) apparently goes straight into your hip joints and clogs them up. One afternoon in the sauna I heard two ostentatiously thin models discussing this problem. "If I *touch* the pâté, my body will rebel," said one. "Mine, too," sighed the other. "At midnight I'll still be able to do the lotus—but not the *bound* lotus."

Frankly, I picked up some of my best diet tips in the whirlpool, where, on any given day, one could soak up a conversation on low-cal, no-carb, high-bulk or mucusless eating—and once in a while a stern lecture on simply not eating. It's not called fasting; it's called cleansing. That's so you'll feel less depressed when you do it.

The whirlpool was also where I first heard about chorionic gonadotropin, a magical substance extracted from the urine of pregnant women, which is said, by its fans, to be the *ne plus ultra* for overweights. There's a clinic that will inject this potion into your buttock six times a week, plus a take-out order of all the food you can eat for 500 calories. The whole deal costs a mere $500 a month, but I hear the string beans vinaigrette are lousy.

Outside the shower, where the scale is, I met a small, intense girl who ate Mallomars every night and then came in mornings to plead with the scale. "Hi, scale," she'd whisper endearingly. "Nice scale . . ." and then she'd get on and off until it registered a number she could live with. I swear she talked it down at least two and a half pounds every time. "What is she, crazy?" someone scoffed one day. "People talk to plants, right?" snapped the Mallomar girl. "I talk to scales."

Then there was the professional dancer who always came in wearing exotic clothes made of chamois dust rags tied together with shoelaces, and children's Fruit of the Loom undershirts. This person claimed she had never dieted a day in her flamboyant life, but came to the club at noon every day for a quart of celery juice followed by an hour of heavy sweating in the steam bath. Very thin she was, but a little wobbly.

I wish I could remember who first touted me onto nuts and raisins. *Fantastically* cleansing, whoever it was promised. The lecithin lady at the front desk was horrified. "You'll put on ten pounds in a week," she predicted. Actually I only put on five and it took almost a month, during which time I felt not only fantastically cleansed but also sublimely happy. What's not to be happy when you're knocking back a quart jar full of roasted cashews, almonds, filberts, Brazils, monukka raisins, pumpkin seeds and sunflower kernels?

But five pounds was five pounds, and in desperation I sought out the girl who ran the juicer in the snack bar. "Angel," I pleaded over a bowl of bean sprouts, "what is there left for me to eat?"

"You have a problem with your carbs, isn't it?" she asked. I said yes.

"Still, you crave fruits and vegies, isn't it?" I said yes.

"Me too!" she exclaimed. "Trust me! Eat only your low-carb fruits and vegies; take no cheese but farmer cheese; and above all, *watch out for pears.* I never have a pear unless I share."

"Never a pear unless I share," I murmured gratefully. "Bless you, Angel."

The following week I met Angel carrying a grocery bag that contained a six-pack of beer, a loaf of sourdough bread . . . and several large green pears.

"Beer?" I cried incredulously. "Bread? *Pears?* Oh, Angel, how could you? I trusted you. I thought you had a carb problem, like me!"

"*Carb* problem?" she echoed, as if I had just coined the phrase. "Forget carbs. Forget problems. Eat whatever is in season, for surely that is what Nature intended, isn't it?"

"But . . . what about *pears?*" I stammered. "What about 'Never a pear unless I share'?"

"Well, *sure!*" said Angel, biting into the largest, juiciest one and handing it to me. "It's *nicer* to share!"

Nuts and raisins. Raisins . . . and *nuts*!, isn't it?

THE SCALE:
Or, You Show Me Yours

If persons with bodily infections are excluded from the club pool by order of the Board of Health, I can think of a number of other persons who should be excluded from using the scale, as a matter of principle. These persons are, namely:

Those who look over your shoulder when you are weighing.

Those who push the indicator down five pounds from their true weight in an effort to mislead the person next in line.

Those who weigh less than a hundred pounds, and who deliberately leave the big weight on fifty, so that the next person feels worse than usual.

Those who proclaim loudly that they have just come from their doctor's office, and that this scale is ten pounds light.

CALISTHENICS:
Or, Last in an Abdominal Series

Breathe in . . .

I don't care what you say, there is something stirring about a calisthenics class. All those thighs smacking together, the hips rolling in unison, legs in the air, scissoring, scissoring, beads of sweat coursing down virtuous brows, and the smug look on the faces of those who go through the entire abdominal series and live to tell the tale.

One tries to stand nonchalantly at the door for a while—just looking, thank you. But inside, one seethes. You know you

CONFESSIONS OF A HEALTH-CLUB NUT · 141

belong in there, don't you? Flat on your allegedly weak back for a count of ten—no, twenty. Limbs lifting and lowering smoothly to the unbearable strain of toneless stomach muscles. In your heart you know you belong in there, but you hover outside, trying to tough it out, sucking in your belly and pretending that's where it always is. Trying with desperate cunning to put it off another day. Tomorrow you'll start calisthenics. Surely three sit-ups on the old slant board are enough for today. No? Well, how about another quick run on the old Jog-a-Matic? And isn't your back still out from lugging those heavy grocery bags last night? What was *in* those bags, anyway? And where is it now? Uh-huh. Well, you'll definitely start calisthenics tomorrow. Today you only came for a sauna. By cab.

And so, sooner or later, depending on when you catch your profile in the club's fifty-two wall-to-wall mirrors, you succumb. You go in there and give your body up to the tender mercies of a lithe, sadistic girl who looks like a social director at an upstate resort, and who sounds like a boot-camp drill sergeant leading a forced march. She's yelling, "Out and in! Point and kick! Lift and lower! Twist and reach!" And you're up on all fours doing leg lifts and thigh swings, and hating yourself, and hating her, and hating most of all the person next to you who did the whole abdominal series without the rest stops, and whose stomach was already flat before she brought it in here.

There was one tiny blond middle-aged lady in my class who came in every day and did her own custom-designed routine of murderous kicks and rolls, two-way stretches, four-way splits and jackknives held for a count of five, all at a pace that resembled a speeded-up comedy film, and who managed to look like a seated duchess while marching back and forth on her absolutely minimal gluteus maximus. Even the teacher couldn't keep up. Once I huffed over to this lady after class and asked her, straight out, "How can you *stand* doing that every day?" She shrugged. "I've been doing it every day of my adult life."

So that was the secret. If only I had an adult life, maybe I could do it too.

After six weeks of intensive effort, I noticed that my stomach had begun to stick out slightly farther than it had when I started. It was firmer, all right, but it definitely stuck farther out.

"Why is that?" I asked my teacher after class, indicating the trouble spot.

"Because," she explained briskly, "you've built up the abdominal muscles right under the abdominal fat."

"Oh," I said. That was the day I quit calisthenics.

. . . And breathe out.

Well, now you know almost everything, except for a few squalid details, like how I bruised both my pelvic bones swiveling on the ledge of the pool during hydrocalisthenics. And how, when I was showing my husband the karate snap-kick, I forgot to take off my clogs. And what my new yoga teacher said when I failed to gather my fragmented mind by concentrating between the eyebrows.

Listen, on second thought, maybe you'd better forget what I told you about that health club. My membership expires in the fall, and I just heard about a terrific new place that offers advanced T'ai Chi, waterbed massage and a thermodynamic exercycle system . . .

The Year of the Barbara

IT WAS NEVER EASY BEING A BARBARA. IN FACT, WHEN THE ANCIENT Greeks first thought up the name, they used it to insult strangers who couldn't speak the language elegantly.

Eons have passed since then, and Barbaras are still working on a snappy rejoinder. This was to have been the year they finally made it: the year of the Barbaras—even of those who lacked the required number of *a*'s to spell it right.

God knows they were off to a promising start. First there was the Jordan barbara, gentle lady from Texas, who set the country on its charmed ear with the force of her orotundity. Even an ancient Greek would have had a word for how she spoke the language: elegantly. When she announced that what was new and wonderful in our Bicentennial political picture was that Barbara was in it, was there one among us who doubted her? Did we think that what we had here was a mere keynote addresser? No, by Hera, we knew. What we had here was probably the first barbara attorney general. Unless it was the first barbara Supreme Court Justice. Well, at the very least, a barbara ambassador to the UN—just to tide us over until she was ready for the number-two spot. A barbara veep? Well, what Socrates didn't know can't hurt him now.

Then came the Streisand barbra *(sic)*, a star who was born again in the shape of an executive movie producer. Also in the shape of a composer, a designer, possibly even a director. Definitely the first of her name and hairdo to exercise total artistic control over her own vehicle. Which was to say, the first fully accredited barbara driver in Hollywood.

Rounding out the illustrious B list was none other than the Walters barbara, transformed from a humble Ms. morning-star into a prime-time name to be reasonered with. This, we were told, was a barbara who could, single-handedly and for a nominal multimillion-dollar consideration, force an entire male-dominated profession to lop off the suffix "man" from its top-job description. Henceforth and forever after, every John, Walter and Harry of them would be lowered from an "anchor-man" to a trimmer, lighter-weight "anchor."

It was so clear that barbarapower was the energy source of the future that even England began rumbling about a possible barbara prime minister. *England?* For one shining moment, there seemed no way to stop them.

So what, does one suppose, happened?

Well, first the Jordan barbara was not named general, or supreme, let alone vice, anything. Indeed, her keynote was still resonating when her name suddenly disappeared from every list of those "under consideration" even for third deputy assistant underling of the department of maybenextyear. Did she contract laryngitis? Was she flu-shot by a swine? Had she perhaps turned up at the wrong convention—in Philadelphia? Not at all. The ancient Greeks in charge of these matters had simply decided that she spoke *their* language inelegantly, after all.

Soon after that, the Streisand barbra drove her shiny new vehicle, with all its lights, horns and music on, out of Hollywood—and smack into a wall of ancient Greek critics. They said she could not steer straight, that she hogged the wheel, that she put her foot down too hard on the accelerator; that her face looked too big in the rear-view mirror, her passengers were nervous and upset, and she didn't know how to work her power-drive button. The Greeks in charge of these matters agreed that a barbra might have rhythm, but that as a moviemaker she could never speak the language elegantly.

Finally, the Walters barbara appeared in a regular evening-news slot, and opened her mouth. "What does that barbara think she is doing?" mumbled a fellow anchor. "Can't she tell that anchoring is no job for a barbara?" Her co-anchor began complaining to the ancient Greeks in his network that other Greeks were making fun of him for sitting next to a barbara who was trying to talk their language in a regular evening-news slot. A chorus of newspaper ancients chimed in sympathetically. Ratings are not up, they chanted, in an ominous minor key. Who will take the evening news seriously if it is reported in the voice of a barbara? Why doesn't she bow out gracefully, before the country stops believing in the power and authority vested in anchors? A great many Greeks in charge of these matters agreed that while a barbara could probably "hostess" an interview, there was no way she could possibly speak the elegant language of the evening news.

Analysts have tried to probe the phenomenon of the great Barbara year, and why it's going so badly. It couldn't be just that barbaras were becoming famous and making big money. Surely barbaras have become famous and made big money before—as models, movie stars, cosmetics queens, dolls and even Greek chorus girls. On the other hand, not many barbaras have ever tried that other ancient Greek game—power, or as they called it, a piece of the π. We have never witnessed such a historic plague of barbaras who wanted to tell the Greeks—in their own language—to go trim their budgets, or their titles, or their armies. We have never had a barbara who could order a Greek to stop bugging his staff, or change his laws, or rewrite his screenplay in *her* language. One imagines that the ancients in charge of these matters must have clutched their very togas at the inelegant prospect of it all.

One hears there are still dangerous pockets of barbaritis in the hills. It is true that the Jordan still sits quietly in Congress, waiting to be called on. At the movie houses, the Streisand racks up an estimated $30 million gross. (Her vehicle also sweeps the Golden Globe awards, from foreign critics who apparently do not understand a word of ancient Greek.)

And on TV, the Walters holds her own, even though her co-anchor tries to pretend she isn't there. More women and young viewers keep tuning in, possibly because they have not done their ancient Greek homework.

Recently a woman journalist who once dropped an anchor herself (even though her name is not Barbara) boldly suggested that maybe the Walters' co-anchor ought to bow out instead. That way he wouldn't have to sit next to her any more.

Nobody, however, goes so far as to suggest that perhaps all the ancient Greeks should bow out and be replaced by barbaras. This of course would instantly lower the status, the salaries, the power and the authority of governing, movie-making and anchoring—down to where they all should have been eons ago. Elegant? Well, Zeus would probably hate the idea, but I daresay the Delphic Oracle warned him. I forget her name, but I think it began with a B.

Letter to a Robber

LISTEN, I HOPE YOU WON'T THINK I'M NOT GRATEFUL FOR THE WAY you handled it. I mean not killing us or . . . anything. How often does a New York holdup man burst into a brownstone on a quiet Saturday night, tie up a whole family, stuff all their cash and valuables into a couple of jumbo shopping bags, and then quietly sashay out into the rain, breaking stride only to select a nice umbrella from the hall rack? As the police put it, ten minutes after you left, "Count your blessings, folks." We have, we have. So, many thanks from all of us—me and Bob and the kids. We'll never forget you.

Did you know you were our first armed robber? Oh, we've had *burglaries*. And both Tony and Roger, who are in their teens, have been shaken down for quarters in the park. But you were absolutely the first person ever to force his way into our house with an actual gun, herd us into an upstairs bedroom, tie us up with pantyhose from my underwear drawer, and spend an hour ransacking the premises, all the while muttering ominously, "Where's the *good* stuff?"

So naturally we had no preconceived idea of what you might have planned in the way of an ending.

It came as a real surprise, when I finally broke loose from my trussed-chicken pose (in yoga class we call it the bow), that not only had you snuck out like, well, a thief in the night, but that except for the severed phone, the torn pantyhose and the lock you had tried to jimmy before Roger opened the door by mistake, you hadn't *destroyed* a thing. I mean, I've seen more physical damage done at a dull cocktail party.

I don't know what I might have done differently if I had suspected, even for a minute, that we would all live to tell about it. From the instant you appeared in the hall, with the gun cradled in your palm like a Master Charge card, it never occurred to me that you weren't going to kill us. "This is it," I said to myself, with the deadly calm of a recorded announcement. And then I added, "So be it." It never guesses, that kind of an inner voice; it knows.

One of the troubles with being a writer is that whenever something unthinkable happens, I can't do anything *but* think about it. It's as if I have no control over the denouement until I get to my typewriter. That night, I realize, the odds were no better than 50–50 that I'd ever make it to my typewriter again. But in the thirty seconds or so that we all stood in the hall like statues, I never thought of *that.* I thought of about a hundred other insanely relevant questions. What made the Jews line up for the gas chamber? Was Hamlet really a simple coward? If I ran for the door, or the telephone, what would you do to Roger, who was standing right next to you? And the more I thought, the more solidly I froze. Could catatonia during a crisis be just a severe form of writer's block? Or was it an elaborate protective device, like an internal Holmes security system? It couldn't stop disaster from striking; it could only keep me from striking back. No heroics. But, you have to admit, no hysterics either. I kept my cool, which kept the children cool, which kept *you* cool. Somehow, some miraculous how, you didn't hurt us. So I must have been doing nothing right. Right?

Anyway, while you were taking over our lives, the writer part of my frozen brain was the only part that didn't get taken. Crouched in its insulated corner, biting its ragged nails, it sat there watching, listening, with a perverse and impotent fascination. It was part prisoner, part voyeur. It could make no move to interfere with our fate. It could only fix the nightmare on my inner ear and eye, to be exorcised later—if I ever woke up.

Well, that was one theory I had about why I began at once to obey your orders; why I moved so slowly and carefully, as if I were swimming underwater or under deep hypnosis. "Lie down," you said softly. I did—and the children followed me. "Don't look up." I didn't; they didn't. Simon says . . . put your hands behind your back. Simon says . . . keep cool; no crying. Simon says let's not play any games.

Of course you didn't tell us to do anything *hard.* You never once forced my hand by threatening, or hurting, the children, by assaulting them or me sexually, by forcing us to help you trap my husband, who was late coming home from an overnight trip to Pittsburgh. And you asked only reasonable questions, in a quiet, reasonable tone. Hypnotic. "Where's your pocketbook?" "Where's your jewelry?" "What airport is your husband coming from?" "Where's the light switch in the closet?"

Only once did I even get angry—and you'd never guess what did it. "What does your father do for a living?" you asked the children. Suddenly my liberated female consciousness flared. Talk about irony! There I was, flat on the floor, a living symbol of woman as victim, and all I could think was: "You rotten chauvinist! Couldn't you ask what their *mother* does? It so happens I've got a book coming out next month!"

And that, of course, started me brooding about being a dead author on the spring list. Ah. I pictured the somber, lump-in-the-throat publisher's ad, with the heavy black border. I imagined the tender posthumous reviews. Hell, I started *writing* them in my head. One for the daily, one for the Sunday . . . oh, victimhood would have its pitiful rewards. For a few crazy minutes there I forgot all about you, rummaging methodically in the bowels of our house. Rifling my office desk? Scattering papers from Bob's file cabinet? Emptying the children's toy chests? Then suddenly you were back in the bedroom, looming over us. But you'd already *done* the bedroom. You'd searched every last drawer, every closet, under the bed, behind the pictures, looking for the "good stuff." There could be only one thing you'd come back for . . .

This is it, I thought, freezing again. This is *really* it. One bullet in the back of each bowed head? The black boots came closer; first the left, then the right, stepped over our prostrate bodies. A single thrill of pure physical terror jolted through my spine. This *is* it!

But all you did was step over us to get to the phone and cut the wire. Why hadn't I guessed by now what you were hanging around for? Waiting for Bob! All the time I thought you'd want to *avoid* him. I kept warning you he was due any minute, *overdue*; thinking it would scare you into hurrying up and getting out. I guess I'd make a lousy robber. Overcautious. You figured what's another half-hour compared to another full wallet? Besides, it was raining out. I had to think about how I could do something *besides* think. But for the life of me, for the life of all of us, I couldn't.

I glanced at Roger, lying there so unnaturally still beside me, his lips chalky with fear. And Tony, a few feet away, seemed half asleep, his small chin buried in the dark carpet. You had taken off his glasses and laid them gently on the floor beside him. But you hadn't hurt him. He and Roger were both alive, and so was I, and you'd left the room again, and maybe, just maybe, the worst was over, and you'd go away, and Bob would be home and it would be tomorrow.

"Roger," I whispered idiotically, "don't ever open the door to a stranger." Roger nodded gravely. Less than an hour ago, at the sound of keys in the front door, Roger had opened the door for Daddy. Only it had turned out to be you instead.

"Did he cut the phone?" I whispered. Roger couldn't see it. Tony was lying closer to it but he couldn't see it either, without his glasses. "Don't try anything, Mommy," Roger pleaded. "He'll shoot us!" My turn to nod gravely. I gave up struggling with the bonds on my wrists and ankles. They only pulled tighter when I writhed, anyway, and the tighter they pulled, the more they hurt. You had let me off easy, tying me up like that. I didn't have to feel guilty for *not* trying—though of course I did. The female role! Oh God, I took to it like a born woman!

Then I heard your steps behind me again, walking back and forth. Pacing? Nervous? Checking us for false moves? No. You were—I still can't believe this—trying on clothes. *My* clothes. Parading back and forth in front of the full-length mirror. All we could see were different colors of suede and leather pants legs flashing past our heads. If only I'd had the nerve to look up, I might have seen the fashion show of the year. But I didn't have the nerve, so I missed it. I bet you look terrific in the violet sheepskin outfit you chose. And the brown leather pantsuit too. I'm still not sure about the fox coat, though. Well, maybe for evening.

"Your husband's kinda late, isn't he?" you said suddenly in that ominously quiet voice. "Uh, yes." I felt a barely controllable urge to start apologizing—"Well, after all, he wasn't expecting you." Or, "Don't feel you have to wait, I'll tell him you were here."

I could tell you were getting edgy. I could hear you crackling paper bags—packing up. What if Bob decided to stay another night in Pittsburgh? *Nobody* stays another night in Pittsburgh. Yes, but what if he had to? If he didn't show up, would you blow your cool, finally, and shoot us, after all? There was definitely a testy note to your voice the next time you asked where the safe was, with the "good stuff." "There is no safe," I said for perhaps the fifth time. I still didn't dare point out that the drawerful of jewelry you'd already emptied *was* the good stuff. Not good enough, apparently. Well, at least we had the same taste in clothes.

As for cash, there wasn't a cent left in the house except for $3 of Roger's allowance, which he had in his pocket. Unfortunately you finally got around to asking if the kids had any money, say, in a piggy bank. Roger instantly piped up about the $3, and told you which pocket. Now we were all wiped out.

And then the doorbell rang. My one chance to throw you off guard! I knew it had to be Bob, but *you* didn't. "Who would that be?" you asked. I was so floored by your syntax that I forgot to lie. "That would be my husband," I parroted like an apt pupil. Judas! Idiot! By the time I realized what I'd done, you were thundering down the stairs to greet him. I heard the two voices—quiet, reasonable, unbelievably controlled—on the landing below. I should have guessed Bob would try to reason with you. A psychiatrist is a psychiatrist even at a time like this. I heard him say, "Maybe I can help you," and I heard you scoff, "How can you help me?" I doubt if any psychiatrist could have come up with the right answer. Seconds later you were both in the bedroom, Bob's hands already tied behind his back. All you had to do was secure his feet, and you were off again. Downstairs? *Gone?* I looked sheepishly at Bob. He was furious. *Furious!* He'd already started struggling violently against the bindings. He had to do *something*—fight, run, something. The absolute antithesis of me! I would have stayed trussed up for another hour, just to be sure you were safely home in a taxi before I moved. Bob strained so hard to be free—to regain control—that he cut deep gashes in his hands and wrists. "Why?" I cried. "What can you possibly do? The phone is cut. He's still in the house!"

"I'll run out!" Bob said. "I'll get help!"

"But he's armed," I argued. "What if he's on the stairs? He'll . . ."

"I think it's a fake gun." (Did he *really* think that? Then why hadn't he tried to stop you? Maybe he thought the gun was real when you pointed it at him, but then decided it was fake because you hadn't shot it?)

I was—and still am—*positive* it was real. Yet I rolled over to help untie Bob's wrists, with the free fingers of my own bound hands. I still don't know why I did that. Because he was so angry? Why *was* he so angry, anyway? Because you had rendered him impotent—unmanned him—with a gun he didn't believe in? You rendered me impotent too—unwomanned me?—but it hadn't made me angry. Certainly not angry enough to risk running into you on a dark staircase.

I was thunderstruck by the contrast between our reactions. Bob was a solid mass of rage and movement. I was a blob of passive ice. Both of us locked into sex-role stereotypes. Culturally induced? Innate? My God, was this whole horror story reducible to a feminist issue? Was *everything* reducible to a feminist issue? What does your father do, indeed? He *acts,* while your mother lies there *thinking.*

Within five minutes Bob was free and running down the stairs, and I had suddenly come to life—untied my wrists, locked the bedroom door and hobbled to the window—just in time to see him running back into the the house. Where were you at that historic moment? None of us knew, but of course you were already gone. Singin', I daresay, in the rain. I never reflected, until days later, on how come I was able to work myself free so fast, *after* Bob did it? Did I feel *protected?* Did I need to have a *man* lead the way? What did that prove about me? About women in general? Nothing, dammit. I know a woman who grappled with a mugger on a dark street and frightened him off. (She also rides a motorcycle.) I consoled myself with the possibility that I might have been braver too (more reckless?) if the children hadn't been there. But how do I know for sure?

Anyway, the nightmare is over. We've followed the cops' sage advice and counted our blessings a fair number of times by now. Also we've absorbed some lessons from the experience. What lessons? Well, the children learned not to open the door without asking who's there, even if they're 1,000 percent *sure* who, as the politicians say. Also, they learned that real violence isn't quite the same as in crime stories. As Roger observed the other day, "In a story, we'd have gotten loose just like that, and sneaked up behind him and given him a karate chop. It sure isn't that easy, is it?"

Bob learned that there are some situations even a psychiatrist can't talk his way out of. When I asked him if he'd learned anything else, he said, "Sure. Never come home late from Pittsburgh."

As for me, I learned to trust the inside of my head, for perhaps the first time in my life. Whatever madness was going on in there—woman's intuition, writer's block, rank cowardice, maternal instinct, death wish, gallows humor, none or all of the above—I now know that it helped save our lives.

I learned that there are feminists in foxholes.

And finally I learned that even if a person practices yoga every day, she cannot remain in the bow position for an hour without feeling stiff in the hip joints. *Scared* stiff.

P.S. By the way, if you're ever in the neighborhood again, don't forget: *You've already been here.*

Queasy Rider

RANDOM THOUGHTS WHILE BEING TOWED THIRTY MILES ALONG Northern State Parkway at midnight in a battered ten-year-old VW squareback, with a sleepy child and a scared cat in my lap:

Janet Guthrie is the first woman driver about whom there are no jokes, even when she has engine trouble.

My friend Merithew, who was raised in California, where only cars are truly happy, is herself truly happy only in cars. She describes them as if they were jewelry or ex-lovers, gives them pet names, and has been known to flirt shamelessly with elderly convertibles old enough to be her trade-in. Last Christmas I gave Merithew a whole fleet of shiny foreign limousines (chocolate, wrapped in colored foil). An hour later, she was hungry for a Mustang.

Lately the media are filled with sad stories of the death of cars—or, rather, the death of America's long, torrid love affair with cars. As usual, they don't mean American *women's* love affair. Except for a few scattered Merithews, women never had time to carry on with their cars. Marriages of convenience were what we had with them. Stolid, boring relationships with big lummoxes that didn't understand us but only wanted to litter our lives with torn coloring books, right sneakers, abandoned bubble gum and the detritus of suburban Lords & Taylors.

Only in California, and maybe in an outpost in upper Westchester, were there women like Merithew for whom the car was a racy alternative life style—a wheel of fortune that promised freedom, or at least a little alienation. I will probably never erase the image of playwright Jean Kerr "escaping" to her parked car and locking herself up in it in order to write humor about suburban family life. Nor that of Tuesday Weld as the distracted movie heroine of *Play It As It Lays,* speeding aimlessly along empty roads ironically named "freeways." I remember she stopped once at a glass-walled highway phone booth that seemed to grow like a transparent weed in a surreal Rousseau landscape. She stopped there to check with her answering service. There were, of course, no messages.

Similarly, all of last year my old friend Megan celebrated her midlife crisis in her car. For months the telephone in her house rang unanswered during the day. "Where do you go?" I kept asking her. Finally she told me: "I drive around."

A recent episode in *Mary Worth,* the ultrareactionary comic strip that rankles first with the feminists, starred a helpless woman driver who was about to fall in love with a garage mechanic. She met him while stalled and terrified on a lonely road. The irresistible thing about him was that not only did he not attack her, he actually told her truthfully that her engine was flooded. "It's a good thing for us women," she gushed later, "that men know everything."

In the fifties the car became a status symbol; in the sixties a sex symbol; in the seventies a violence symbol. There was even a horror movie called *The Car.* Hollywood does have a way of casting all its aging sex symbols as evil old crones.

Whatever Happened to Baby Chrysler? Too old for romantic leads, but she can still gnash her grillwork and run a mean car chase.

Is it politically important that I can think of only one daredevil movie car chase in which a woman driver not only won but didn't crack up? It was in *The Late Show;* Lily Tomlin was at the getaway wheel, and Art Carney sat stoically nursing his ulcers in the death seat while she gleefully demolished an entire neighborhood. I remember thinking that the sequence should be shown to every husband who ever complained about teaching a wife to drive—especially the fellow who does those obnoxious TV commercials for the Automobile Club of America.

Janet Guthrie notwithstanding, I'm beginning to think they will never liberate car ads. The slinky, elegant model still matches the upholstery and looks as if she comes with the machine, as an optional extra. Sometimes they pose her outside, or stretched out on top, like an oversized hood ornament. If they go so far as to put her behind the wheel, her pose makes it clear that she's just idling there, with her motor purring in neutral. The customer is always *Mr.* Right.

Once in a while, in the old days, the heroine used to drive her own snappy roadster. She was a spoiled, rich, high-spirited girl like Grace Kelly or Katharine Hepburn, and she always drove too fast on dangerous roads, symbolically daring the hero (Cary Grant) to slow her down and take over. You could tell he was a hero if he liked her spirit, but managed to steer her home in the end. Driving was a metaphor for control, mastery, independence and power. In the ads, it still is—and women still don't have it.

The only car I ever really loved was also the first one I ever owned—a turquoise-blue used Chevy convertible with a white canvas top and a stick shift. Knowing how to shift gears and change a tire was very important to me; almost as important as not knowing how to type with ten fingers. (For a newspaper reporter, it was a sign of weakness if you couldn't type sixty words a minute with two fingers. I still type that way, and I still drive a car with a gearshift, though I suspect neither skill has the same cachet any more.)

Pamela doesn't love her car with the unbridled passion of a Merithew, but she does get a kick out of driving. I asked her whether it was a power or an adventure kick, and she said "Both." Passing a car on the highway excites her, but so does driving along a leafy country road, executing graceful, lyrical turns. She thinks of it as a kind of music: Mozart on the radio, Pamela at the wheel.

Hildy, my friend in advertising, thinks that if women had been running the government at the turn of the last century, America might never have gone the route of private cars or flush toilets.

Women, she says, would have opted for mass transit (more sociable) and the ecocycle for waste disposal (less mechanical trouble). Think of it: women might have kept James Bond out of his Aston-Martin DB III. Jimmy Carter might never have made an impression by walking to his inauguration. Nothing would have driven us to drive-ins, trapped us in radar, designed our early sex lives around (and under) a steering wheel, or parked us on alternate sides of the street.

No stand-up comic would have cracked wise about his wife totaling the garage. No Mafioso would ever have kissed a godfather goodbye with a flick of his ignition key. No cowboy singing star would have died in the back of a chauffeured limousine. Janet Guthrie would never have had engine trouble in the Indy 500.

And I would never have had to be towed thirty miles along Northern State Parkway in a battered ten-year-old VW squareback—the sort of experience which leads women drivers to reckless thinking about cars.

Ms. Alliances

I never bother with people I hate;/That's why the lady is a tramp.
—LORENZ HART

I HEAR A PENDULUM SWINGING. TOPLESS ENTERTAINMENT MAY lose some of its license; homosexual rights are wronged; a Wisconsin judge finds rape "normal" in a permissive world, only to find himself strictly overruled by an outraged community. We'll be back with these and other stories in a minute.

Meanwhile, my friends are whispering again: "Is this good or bad for women?" As usual, the answer is "Of course."

The other day I sat in a roomful of illustrious feminists who were meeting to discuss the latest pornography blight, and the latest radical cure for it. Street actions? Referendums? A $10,000 ad explaining the feminist stance on porn (It isn't sex we're against—it's anti-woman violence)? Well, how about a national group called "Save Our Women, Inc."? I said seriously, "I wish we had Anita Bryant on our side."

There was an audible gasp and scattered hollow laughter. Surely I was kidding. Anita Bryant?! Among feminists these days, that's a four-letter, fighting word. One of the women, an activist for homosexual rights, shook her head in dismay. If I was kidding, it was Not Funny.

Another woman suggested that perhaps what I had meant —if I had actually *meant* anything—was only that Anita Bryantism is awesomely effective; that feminists might need to learn the secret of that kind of effectiveness if we are ever to win our own battles. We could, after all, also use the secret formula of Marabel Morganism–Phyllis Schlaflyism too, for that matter. One suspects that they are all the same. All of these women know (or are carefully taught) which emotional buttons to push, and when and how hard to push them.

Well, that was certainly part of what I meant, though nowhere near all. I tried to explain away the shock: Of course I deplore what "that woman" stands for; of course I stand against her. But the "Bryant constituency" is ours too, at least some of the time. We even have identical goals in some crucial areas—pornography, violence, wife-battering, child abuse. So wouldn't it help if we could begin, finally, to see—and to use —the connection?

All around that room, there were murmurs of protest. Not out of anger, but profound discomfort. Not because we didn't all sense the urgent need to "broaden our base" for some of our toughest causes, but simply because most of us couldn't imagine playing any kind of sexual politics in which the likes of Anita Bryant became our bedfellows. Where we diverge is too sharp; where we meet or overlap, too slippery. Yet some leaders of the fight against child pornography are also "right-to-lifers." A leader of the fight to clean up Times Square is against ERA. John Birchers are for freedom of choice in medical treatment; so is the women's health movement. And church groups may join a feminist outcry against sexual abuse, though *they* mean everything but "man and wife" in the missionary position. Remarkably, even Anita Bryant's phalanx of enemies—male and female homosexuals, and their supporters—diverge sharply over gay male attacks on her as a woman, and lesbian-feminist "trashing" of her as a "straight" woman.

At the meeting, heads were still shaking, however. Passing references to Puritans and witch hunts were made, along with a chilling reminder that *"we* are the witches."

Finally Robin Morgan, the poet and author, reached for the common chord. "Women who love their children," she began, "women who are deeply religious, they don't feel at one with us. They aren't even aware that we share any of their feelings. I can just hear their astonishment: 'You mean you feminists love your *kids*? You mean *you're* against smut?' The fact is, Anita Bryant can reach and move those women—but we can't."

I nodded gratefully, suddenly remembering a recent encounter with a woman I don't know well, and whose politics and life style are vastly different from my own. At a party she said that she felt closer to me lately, and I asked her why. "Because I realize you're not a feminist," she said, "—you're a woman." I didn't contradict her because I understood what she meant. She had simply begun to see more of the bonds between us, and to focus less on the divisions. I knew there was a lesson in there somewhere.

There are other lessons we could be learning, too. The night after that meeting I saw *Godfather II* on Home Box Office, and also read a book called *The Managerial Woman*. Both were filled with the sobering images of determined men getting where they want to go by doing business with their sworn enemies—or else. Ethnic-slurring U.S. senators and proud Mafia dons. Pragmatic industrialists and greedy military dictators. Big wheelers and dirty dealers. Godfather II, like Godfathers I, III and the whole bloody Family, may be the quintessential American male self-portrait for the seventies; a riveting photograph of the essential amorality that supports his American-dream twins, "Family" and "Winning." Besides, it looks a lot like the evening news.

Feminists are hardly godfathers (or mothers) in training; nor do we want to be. But we do want power; we do want to win. And we do need to be aware of what it takes. Obviously I don't mean murder; nor do I mean betrayal, corruption, selling out or compromising who we are and what we are about. All I mean is what, in the business world, is called flexibility—the knack of dealing with the realities of the environment.

If *Godfather II* is a photograph, *The Managerial Woman* is an X-ray. The authors, two women Ph.D.'s who work as management consultants for major corporations, offer a matter-of-fact diagnosis of what makes men tick politically, while women still don't have the rhythm. Something to do with tolerating, putting up with, and using, the people one can't stand. Men start doing it when they are children, the day they learn it takes eleven to make a football team, and nobody can find ten other kids he really likes. He's got to choose: play only with friends—or play football.

Girls—those solitary skaters, gymnasts, swimmers, pick-up-sticks players—never learn to make that necessary adjustment. So they grow up thinking they don't *have* to play ball with anyone who isn't their friend. They also grow up thinking that enemies who shake hands over bargaining tables and start helping each other are hypocrites. Even when the shaking of those hands, and the giving of that help, can mean the difference between winning and losing.

In politics, sexual or otherwise, it matters a lot who won or lost. Which determines how you play the game.

Besides, whatever happened to the old ethical feminism that operated in consciousness-raising groups? We used to come together from very different places—and we came not to judge, destroy, appease or lie to each other, but to find the connective tissues, without ever disowning our differences. Therein used to lie our strength.

So if a woman who was against ERA, against abortion, against homosexual rights, walked into that roomful of feminists and said, "I'm with you on rape, child abuse and pornography; what can I do to help?," could we really afford to cut her dead? I don't think so.

The fact is, she ain't coming to us. If we want her, though, we know where she is. It's up to us to get in touch.

About the Author

Born in New York City, LOIS GOULD is the author of the best-selling novels *Such Good Friends* (1970), *Necessary Objects* (1972), *Final Analysis* (1974) and *A Sea-Change* (1976), and the forthcoming fable *X: A Fabulous Child's Story* (1978). Her previous nonfiction books are *So You Want to Be a Working Mother!* and *The Childbirth Challenge* (with Dr. Waldo L. Fielding). Her short fiction and articles have appeared in many magazines, including *Ms., McCall's* and *New York,* and in the *New York Times.* Ms. Gould is married to Robert E. Gould, M.D., a psychiatrist. They have two sons and a calico cat who is active in the Movement.